The Christian Skeptic

The Christian Skeptic

Caught between Belief and Doubt

JODY SEYMOUR

WITH
GAIL SPACH

RESOURCE *Publications* · Eugene, Oregon

THE CHRISTIAN SKEPTIC
Caught between Belief and Doubt

Wipf and Stock
An Imprint of Wipf and Stock Publishers
199 W. 8th Ave., Suite 3
Eugene, OR 97401

www.wipfandstock.com

ISBN 13: 978-1-62564-985-0

Manufactured in the U.S.A.   02/05/2015

Scripture quotations from the New Revised Standard Version of the Bible are copyright 1989, by the Division of Christian Education of the National Council of the Churches of Christ in the United States of America and are used by permission.

The author gratefully acknowledges permission to include the lyrics of the song "A Different Jesus," by Ed Kilbourne.

Excerpt taken with permission from "Rag-Tag Army" from *The Way of the Wolf,* by Martin Bell. Copyright 1970 by Martin Bell, published by Ballantine Books, New York, New York. All rights reserved. Website: bar-ringtonbunny.com.

"The Nail-Torn God" is excerpted from the book *New Poems: Eighty Songs at Eighty: The Fifth Book of Verse,* by Edwin Markham, Doubleday, Doran & Company, Inc. 1935.

This book is dedicated to the loving memory of Leslie Weatherhead whose book *The Christian Agnostic* was a lifeline thrown to me when I was sinking in a sea of orthodoxy in my younger years. It is also dedicated to those of you who will read it and who need such a lifeline now.

With many thanks to my friend and colleague Gail Spach, who edited this book and elaborated on some of its content. Gail is on staff as our church librarian.

Table of Contents

Preface

A Personal Word of Caution
before Reading this Book

IF YOU HAPPEN TO have picked up this book out of curiosity—or for whatever reason—but you are not at all restless when it comes to matters of religion or faith, I offer this very personal, but very real, word of caution: Put this book down; it is not for you.

My dear wife offers me wisdom from time to time. Once in a while, I listen. She tells me that many people do not have as many questions as I do. She is one of them. She has a simple faith that was nurtured during her Lutheran upbringing, and it is the ground upon which she walks. While she seldom uses God talk, she is constantly doing all kinds of things for people without being asked. As she walks upon the path she follows, she loves and cares for people much better than I do.

My wife's faith instructs her actions without any need for discussion or debate. She does not question life, nor does she see the things of God as being particularly mysterious. She does not like to get involved with a lot of theological wrestling, and she certainly doesn't want anyone, including her minister husband, shaking the ground beneath her. We need, in our fast-paced materialistic culture, more people with a simple faith like hers. Why would I muddy the waters of a faith like that?

So if you are in some way like my wife, in that you do not have a lot of questions, please do both of us a favor and read no further. God makes all kinds of people. I wrote this book as a restless, skeptical Christian, a questioner for other questioners, and if you are not one of those questioners, then that is probably a good thing for both of us.

Secondly, if you have ever been part of a church that I have served as a pastor during the last forty plus years, please stop and hear this: If I have been of help to you, and you do not need to hear the inner rumblings of a person in whom you have placed trust, then put the book down now. Let me remain that one in the robe from whom you have heard the good news and received the sacraments.

I am that person, but I am more. This book is about the more. This effort is offered because I have a deep place in my heart for those who think they are not, or cannot be, part of the Christian faith because they have too many questions and doubts. They think they do not fit. They are uncomfortable with orthodox labels. They have some form of belief but carry with them a lot more unbelief.

In my own struggle to believe, I have discovered some points of light that I want to share with questioning pilgrims on the road. If you do not need such a lantern for the road because it is simply not that dark on your journey, then I celebrate your place along the pilgrimage.

It is my sincere hope that what I have to share will be of help to the person caught somewhere between belief and doubt. I want to make a case for a living faith that is big enough to hold both belief and doubt.

So now I've said it, a loving word of warning for the wise. Thanks for listening, and whether you decide to put down this book or to read on, may God bless you.

Jody Seymour

The Nail-Torn God

Edwin Markham
1852–1940

Here in life's chaos make no foolish boast
That there is any God omnipotent,
Seated serenely in the firmament,
And looking down on men as on a host
Of grasshoppers blown on a windy coast,
Damned by disasters, maimed by mortal ill,
Yet who could end it all with one blast of Will.
This God is a man-created ghost.

But there *is* a God who struggles with the All,
And sounds across the worlds his danger-call.
He is the builder of roads, the breaker of bars,
The One forever hurling back the Curse—
The nail-torn Christus pressing toward the stars,
The Hero of the battling universe.[1]

1. Markham, New Poems, 58.

Introduction

Two Writings That
Helped Save My Faith

I ADMIT THAT I "drank the Kool-Aid" in my youth and, like many others, believed what I was told about the only faith I knew. Perhaps it is a bit too strong to put it that way. After all, this expression comes to us from the tragic story of Jim Jones, who used fear and mind control to shape a whole group of people into thinking his way and acting like robots up until the end. Jones convinced them to give their all, and we are still talking about what a terrible deed he did. An attitude of skepticism and some critical thinking would have served those followers of Jim Jones very well.

I use this extreme expression about drinking Kool-Aid for you, the reader, because if you picked up this book, you probably hold within you two of the key words of its title: *belief* and *doubt*. You believe, but you also experience doubt. As Frederick Buechner points out in his collection of meditations on this theme, this is "some [of us] all of the time and all [of us] some of the time."[1] In this book, I hope to show that having a healthy dose of skepticism can be a good thing for a believer.

When I walked away from the Kool-Aid, there were two pieces of writing that helped save my faith. One of them was Leslie Weatherhead's book, *The Christian Agnostic*, which I have used as a kind of framework for this book. I was a young man beginning ministry in the Christian tradition, but I had a problem. I was in the midst of a crisis because at that critical time in my life, my first year as a pastor,

1. Buechner, *The Hungering Dark*, 15.

I did not believe enough in some of the doctrines that I would be called on to "dispense." I was afraid that I could not run the Kool-Aid stand because I could no longer drink the stuff myself.

When I discovered *The Christian Agnostic*, I was extremely thirsty, having gone cold turkey from the Kool-Aid habit. I found in Weatherhead's book a cup of cold water that refreshed and re-invigorated me. Since this man of great faith wrote for those who were struggling with that faith, and his words were so important to me at that time of my life, I have always considered him to be one of my mentors. I have recommended his book to countless people who, like me, needed a hip replacement. Hold on, I know I am switching from talking about Kool-Aid stands to a medical metaphor, but you will see how this image is relevant to this faith and "un-faith" journey.

The hip image comes from that famous wrestling match in the Hebrew Bible (the book Christians have traditionally called The Old Testament). A rascal named Jacob decided one evening to take on none other than God, who is described in the text as a "mysterious stranger."[2] Biblical scholars and depth psychologists have offered countless interpretations of this wrestling match. Was Jacob really fighting with his internal self and his past? Was this a way to come to terms with his guilt for tricking his elderly father and swindling his brother of his birthright? Or was this a real tug of war with the One who, on last check, created at least a hundred billion galaxies? The answer is "yes." It is "all of the above."

Like many others, I know that to tangle with God is also to tangle with the deepest parts of oneself, and that to do so will often leave one tired and in need of first aid, maybe even surgery. Jacob thought he was getting the upper hand on God, the mysterious stranger, but he discovered that when he walked away, he walked with a limp, one he would never get over. To deal with the real God, rather than the one often advertised by smiling TV preachers, is to dare risk both mystery and change. Weatherhead's book offered me a new chance to rediscover the real God who was, and

2. Genesis 32:22–32.

is, full of mystery, and as I did, I experienced a change in the ways that I perceived that God.

I have always wanted to write a book along the lines of *The Christian Agnostic* in order to share my own wrestling match and to offer some insights to those who desire to walk the path of faith, but for whom the journey seems more like a marathon than a sprint. This book is for those who are intrigued by the Christian faith but who have trouble believing many of the things they feel they ought to believe, those who realize that they need that cup of cold water but who refuse to stop at the Kool-Aid stand.

I have used my mentor's outline to write this book because it will help us reflect on many of those doctrines that seem so essential to the Christian faith but that can be problematic, confusing, or both. I stand in the shadow of Leslie Weatherhead but feel that I have something to offer to the modern reader who, like me, needs to know what to do with some of that unbelief.

Weatherhead's own words from his original introduction are intriguing and provocative. The book may be out of print, having been written in 1965, but I find his words to be as true today as ever. In addressing the fact that many do not attend church because of intellectual difficulties, he goes on to say, perhaps surprisingly, that it is many of these "professing agnostics" that are "nearer belief in the true God than are many conventional church-goers who believe in a bogy that does not exist whom they miscall God."[3]

As I type these words, I am reminded of how refreshing Weatherhead's message was to me as a young minister forty years ago when I was struggling to reconcile my faith with my intellect. He not only described my wrestling match but pointed me in the direction I should go in order to tend my wounded hip. How many times have I referred to his words when I worked with someone who was having trouble with God or, at least, with their concept of God?

It was this author that helped me to realize that I had grown up with an unhelpful and, frankly, unbiblical idea of the nature of God, and I have since discovered that I was not alone in believing in this false God, or "bogy," which is the word Weatherhead used.

3. Weatherhead, *The Christian Agnostic*, 14.

(In writing this book, I'm also using a different style from that of Weatherhead, whose book contains some old-fashioned, male-oriented language and some obscure British terms. Moreover, a few of his ideas, being dated, could use new light.)

Weatherhead's goal was to show that it is possible to be a loyal Christian even if you are agnostic about some of the dogmas and creeds of the faith, hence the title of his book, *The Christian Agnostic*. I am making a similar argument in this book but have used the term "skeptic" rather than "agnostic." Here is how Weatherhead defines a Christian agnostic, and how I would characterize the intended readership of the book you now have in your hands:

> A person who is immensely attracted by Christ and who seeks to show his spirit, to meet the challenges, hardships and sorrows of life in the light of that spirit, but who, though he is sure of many Christian truths, feels that he cannot honestly and conscientiously 'sign on the dotted line' [drink the Kool-Aid—my words] that he believes certain theological ideas about which some branches of the church dogmatize; churches from which he feels excluded because he cannot 'believe.' His intellectual integrity makes him say about many things, 'It may be so. I do not know.'[4]

When it comes to what we know about God, I offer you an analogy in the form of a Food and Drug Administration mandate. It seems that people grew tired of buying food products that they thought to be one thing because of the description on the package only to discover that what was purchased was not what they were expecting. In order to prevent such false advertising, the Food and Drug Administration began requiring that the ingredients of a product be listed on the label in descending order of predominance. In other words, if you purchase a drink called "Apple Fruit Delight" and then read the ingredients, you might discover that apple juice is listed as the third ingredient, following water and high fructose corn syrup. There could actually be less than 1% apple juice in the drink.

4. Ibid., 15.

So, I ask you, what would you find on the ingredients label when it comes to God, or faith in God? I offer you what the Christian skeptic might need to hear. The first ingredient is not power, or omnipresence, or even love, though these are important ingredients. It is mystery. Ask Jacob as he limps away from his wrestling match with God. Ask him to describe what just happened and he will come up empty. All he knows is that his encounter with this mysterious other not only left his hip hurting but his life altered forever.

In Weatherhead's words:

> I believe passionately that Christianity is a way of life, not a theological system with which one must be in intellectual agreement. I feel that Christ would admit into discipleship anyone who sincerely desired to follow him, and allow that disciple to make his creed out of his experience; to listen, to consider, to pray, to follow, *and ultimately to believe only those convictions about which the experience of fellowship made him sure* [Italics mine].[5]

Sounds to me like Weatherhead knew something about the nature of God and Christ before the FDA mandate. It is out of the experience of an encounter with Christ, and the one he called *Abba, Daddy,* that a living theology grows.

It may sound trite to state that the journey is sometimes at least as important as—or possibly more important than—the destination. It is on the journey that we learn and grow. So much of what I was fed, or that I drank, if I stick with the Kool-Aid image (which maybe I should give up), was built around a very exclusivist type of Christianity that was always proclaiming that Jesus is "*the* way," and that all who do not believe in him are lost. Even as a child I wondered why this should be the case. Was God so unimaginative that God could not allow for other ways to find the truth? Jesus said that he was "the way"; he did not say he was the destination. The image of "the way" implies a continuing journey.

A phrase that means a lot to me comes from a poem by T.S. Eliot: "We shall not cease from exploration / and the end of our

5. Ibid., 16.

exploring / will be to arrive where we started / and know the place for the first time."[6] This is, in part, what I hope to allow you, the reader and pilgrim, to do as you explore the ideas in this book. I hope this book will be a journey for you.

I invite you on this journey where you are invited to be a spiritual pilgrim rather than a religious tourist. While a camera-toting tourist is intent on hopping from place to place, seeing as many sights as there are to see, a pilgrim walks slowly, humbly, and with curiosity, unafraid of what may be around the next corner, and seeking truth wherever it may be found.

I like what Weatherhead says:

> Every effort made to express the Christian religion will be full of mistakes and half-truths and there must be large patches of reverent agnosticism in which the seeker is bound to say, 'I just don't know'. . . . But . . . the glorious fact is that the truth cannot be overthrown, and will more and more emerge as man's fearless questing brings him insight.[7]

It is for the purpose of questing after that mystery, the emerging truth, that I invite you, the reader, to join me on a journey. It will be a journey where, taking the time to stop and ponder, we will take another look at the faith called Christian and, hopefully, to come to know it for the first time.

The second writing that helped save my own faith was Edwin Markham's poem, "The Nail-Torn God." I no longer remember exactly when or where I was on my own journey when I first encountered these words, but it was at the right time. "When you are ready to learn, the teacher will come" is a true wisdom saying. I was ready and needed to learn that God was more, not less, than what my religion had taught me.

The God of my childhood was much too small. I was having a hard time breathing the air where God was all knowing and all powerful. Such air was supposed to be life-giving, but I was suffocating in it. The concept of a God who was working out a

---

6. Eliot, "Little Gidding," in *The Norton Anthology of Modern Poetry*, 478.

7. Weatherhead, *The Christian Agnostic*, 21.

plan in every tiny detail was no longer working for me personally nor professionally. In the midst of yet another tragedy where I was called in to comfort a family, I found myself saying to God, "You embarrass me. I am tired of defending you. If this is your plan and you are working things out, then you are not succeeding."

I did not say this publicly. After all, that seemed at the time not to be "good for business." But it was what was on my heart and in my soul. All I can tell you is that somewhere into that same air that was stifling for me, there came a whisper. The whisper said this to me, "I never asked you to defend me. I can take care of myself. Quit trying to figure me out, and simply stand with my hurting children when there are no answers. I am not the God you thought I was, but I am God. Now, get back to work."

When I found "The Nail-Torn God," or better put, it found me, I needed to hear its claim—that an omnipotent God looking down indifferently on humankind in the midst of all the chaos is a "man-created ghost." I also needed to hear the words of hope that conclude the poem, that "there *is* a God who struggles with the All"—"the nail-torn Christus pressing toward the stars, the Hero of the battling universe."[8]

I needed that God. I needed that nail-torn Christ. I no longer needed nor could I profess a God up there who kept some kind of score sheet so that if your life did not "add up" in the end, you got tossed into a waste basket, a garbage can that, by the way, was on fire. I realized that the Christ I encountered in moments of pause was not a Jesus who desired to exclude those who did not believe in him according to certain guidelines. I needed the "nail-torn Christus" who represented a God who was, and is, a "builder of roads and a breaker of bars." I needed a "Hero of the battling universe," and I found that God.

The God I discovered, far from being an indifferent spectator, is passionately concerned about the world, even to the point of vulnerability and pain. I came to understand that God's power is not that of a controlling tyrant directing everything from afar, but more the creative, persuasive, loving, life-giving and liberating

8. Markham, *New Poems*, 58.

power of one who has given freedom to all creation and, at the same time, has charged and empowered us to be participants in this work of building roads and breaking bars.

I want to offer this God to you as we journey together. So as we begin, I give you words that I have shared countless times with people who have come to me hurting because they feel that God has let them down. These are people who thought that they could no longer really be Christian because life had broken them open. Some wondered if they had done something wrong and had brought suffering upon themselves, others decided that God's plan was simply too harsh for them to continue to believe in a micromanaging divine power.

These people needed a nail-torn Jesus, not a judgmental savior who came only to save those who joined the club and knew the secret handshake. I found this Jesus, thanks in part to the words of Markham's poem and the open invitation from Leslie Weatherhead not to give up but to join others who need to hear the good news that agnostics and skeptics are welcome on the journey.

And here is Weatherhead's invitation to you:

> Don't exclude yourself from the fellowship of Christ's followers because of mental difficulties. If you love Christ and are seeking to follow him, take an attitude of Christian agnosticism to intellectual [and, I would add, spiritual] problems at least for the present. Read this book to see if the essentials of the Christian religion are clarified for you and only accept those things which gradually seem to you to be true. Leave the rest in a mental box labeled, 'awaiting further light.' [This is my favorite phrase that I use often for spiritual pilgrims who stumble into my path.] In the meantime, join in with us in trying to show and to spread Christ's spirit, for this, we feel, is the most important thing in the world.[9]

Now, that is a journey I can take. I invite you to come on the journey.

---

9. Weatherhead, *The Christian Agnostic*, 21.

1

What Does Being a Christian Really Mean?

I WOULD LIKE TO think that it is only of late that being a Christian means being right about certain doctrines or ethical guidelines. Unfortunately, the history of that which we call the Christian faith is fraught with debates about "right" practice and belief and litmus tests administered to determine one's worthiness to gain entrance.

The founder of the faith did not administer such tests. Nonetheless, soon after Jesus left his tiny band of disciples, the testmakers union gathered. He had started a movement of people who were simply called "followers of the way," but as soon as someone in a city named Antioch decided that they needed a label, the T-shirt and cap shops started selling items with "Christian" stamped across the front, and it began to be important to be "right."

I think Jesus would particularly like a poem by Yehuda Amichai that is called "From the Place We Are Right." In this poem, Amichai, who is widely regarded as Israel's greatest modern poet, asserts that "flowers will never grow" from the "place where we are right," because that place is "hard and trampled like a yard." In contrast, however, he says that "doubts and loves dig up the world like a mole, a plow," and in that place of humility, "a whisper will be heard in the place where the ruined house once stood."[1]

---

1. Amichai, *The Selected Poetry of Yehuda Amichai*, 34.

The hard and trampled ground of "right" creed and "right" doctrine is often not a place of growth, especially for those who are looking to discover some fertile territory for their journey. So many times the church becomes the battleground for "truth" at the expense of those who are seeking water for thirsty spirits.

My image of the church is that of pipes and plumbing. The plumbing is a means for the water to get to its intended destination, but if we are not careful, we become plumbers who are always tampering with the pipes. We become enamored with the pipes so much that we end up worshiping the twists and turns of the plumbing. All the while, thirsty pilgrims hear the clanging of the pipes and wonder what all the fuss is about. They are looking for water. Instead, we give them a manual of how to understand and adjust the plumbing.

The Spirit of the living God is the water. It flows up from underneath our very lives. The water is always there, available to all of us, but people quickly feel the need to capture and control it. Creeds and doctrines are the pipes. They can be useful in helping get the water to us, but they can also get clogged up and keep us from being able to drink. Jesus came offering cups of cold water to thirsty people and letting us know about the wellspring of water that is always ready to bubble up within us.

There is a plumbing story in the New Testament. Jesus asks a Samaritan woman for some water at a well.[2] He does not ask her to recite any creeds; he asks her for something to drink. In response, she brings to him her doubts and her desire for living water. Jesus, in his usual manner, senses that she needs something, but unless he opens the door, she will not come in. So he does something very human, which he often does, because he is, after all, very human; he asks her to draw him some water.

The conversation immediately becomes one about religion when the woman points out that she is a woman from Samaria and he is a Jew; it is not kosher for a Jewish man to talk with a woman in public, especially a Samaritan—she is considered to be the "wrong" gender and the "wrong" religion. But Jesus does what

2. John 4:7-15.

I believe Jesus does today. He cuts through the pipes and exposes some fresh water for the very thirsty woman to drink. Instead of a test about plumbing, which could very well lead to dissatisfaction and disappointment, Jesus offers himself as living water. Jesus is more concerned about thirsty people finding water than about the specific containers for that water.

Weatherhead's book begins with a section titled "Dissatisfaction and Disappointment." To be a follower of the one who says such things as take up your cross and follow me, deny yourself, love your enemies, forgive seventy times seven, risk being last to be first, and serve and give until it hurts, is not easy and can lead to some dissatisfaction and disappointment when it comes to the happiness and success that are standards for contentment in our culture. Weatherhead's concern, and mine, however, is not this kind of dissatisfaction. He wrote, and I write, for those who feel disappointment and dissatisfaction with what they are told they need to believe in order to be a Christian.

Leslie Dixon Weatherhead was a man ahead of his time. A Methodist minister and President of the Methodist Conference, he lived between 1893 and 1976. He was a very controversial figure because of the way he questioned many of the tenets of the Christian faith. Today he would very probably be glad to find himself in good company. He would most likely now be part of a new movement within the church that is known as *Emergent Christianity*.

Jim Wallis, an evangelical progressive, captures something of this movement in his comment on the cover of a book on Emergent Christianity by Tony Jones. He writes, "The influence of Jesus of Nazareth is moving among a new generation hungry for something real and desperate to move beyond simplistic polarities [left vs. right, liberal vs. conservative, mainline vs. evangelical] inherited from the past."[3]

Brian McLaren, one of the main spokespersons for the Emergent Church, in one of his books, *A Generous Orthodoxy*, describes many of the ideals of this movement: a focus on Jesus Christ as the center of the Christian faith; a generous orthodoxy—straight

3. Jones, *The New Christians*, cover.

thinking tempered by humility, charity, courage and diligence[4]; a missional and social justice emphasis that expresses God's love for the whole world; a high regard for the Bible, which is taken seriously but not literally; respect for other faith traditions; a comfort with uncertainty; and an appreciation for the mystical, the metaphoric, and the poetic.

In this book, McLaren describes how Christian beliefs have changed over the centuries. Beliefs that were considered "right" at one time do not always remain "right." For example, during the medieval era (from the fifth to the fifteenth century), most Christians believed that the earth was fixed and that the sun rotated around it. They didn't think twice about "the divine right of kings, the origin of species . . . how races can and should relate to one another . . . and the standard operating procedures used by the church."[5]

However, during the modern era (which began in the sixteenth century CE and peaked during the Enlightenment period), there was an explosion in scientific knowledge, technological invention, conquests, and discoveries, and the church had to adapt. Martin Luther, in 1517, created ninety-five provocative statements that asked questions about traditional beliefs and invited debate. During this time, Christians increasingly wanted their faith to be objective, rational and scientific. Bible scholars and theologians alike worked on reconciling faith with reason.

In the second half of the 1900s, the modern era gave way to a "new postmodern paradigm of pluralism, relativism, globalism and uncertainty."[6] With an expanding appreciation of other cultures, people began to recognize that there are many different ways of seeing and doing things and that objectivity is not even a possibility. This is the era in which we now find ourselves.

McLaren says that *absolute truth*[7] has not been discounted, but *absolute knowledge* has. People are no longer satisfied with easy answers. There is a renewed interest in a spirituality that is focused

4. McLaren, *A Generous Orthodoxy*, 30.
5. McLaren, *A New Kind of Christianity*, 16.
6. Ibid., 8.
7. McLaren, *The Church on the Other Side*, 166.

on relationships, love, shared discussion, and integrity, and interestingly, a certain disillusion with reason, science and technology as *the only way* of acquiring knowledge. With this paradigm shift, churches are scrambling to try to figure out how to make Christianity work for this new era. Some of those gathering to wrestle with this issue would identify as being part of this *Emergent,* or *Emerging* Christianity.

As I read some of McLaren's books and the overview of Emergent Christianity as compiled by Tony Jones in *The New Christians,* I could see Leslie Weatherhead smiling from the great beyond. Not only do I personally resonate with this movement and its openness to a truly generous orthodoxy, I also reached out to some of those who I sensed were among the "dissatisfied and disappointed." Along with the Rev. Susan Heafner-Heun, I helped birth a new Emergent church community that was sponsored by my own congregation. I see those who belong to this group, which calls itself "Inclusion Community," as the people that Weatherhead wrote for years ago.

Though small, they celebrate that they have found a safe place to share a spiritual journey around what some call *Progressive Christianity.* Some of those who attend tell me that they felt wounded and excluded by the church but they now have discovered a loving and non-judgmental community where different understandings of Jesus are both welcomed and nurtured. Within the Inclusion Community, there is also a deep respect for other faith traditions, something that you do not always find in other Christian denominations, and a strong sense of service to the wider community.

One reason I am writing this book is because of the reaction of some of my peers in ministry to my support and sponsorship of this Inclusion Community. They were truly bothered by it and considered it to be, at best, not really Christian and, at worst, syncretistic and even heretical. When they heard that the call to worship at the Inclusion Community—which by the way does center on Christ—was initiated by the ringing of a Buddha bell, they contacted my bishop to complain that such a practice was, shall

I say, unorthodox, and even dangerous. I should have told those who called me to share their concern that I have many times in my own very traditional congregation used Tibetan prayer bells to center my Christian congregation for worship.

I should also have shared with some of my minister friends my favorite expression written by Peter Berger: "I have not yet found a heresy into which my theological views comfortably fit."[8] Or, I could have mentioned the words of Thomas Huxley, who wrote in 1880, "It is the customary fate of new truths to begin as heresies."[9] The historic heresies, after all, were espoused by those who desired to be followers of Christ. Some of their ideas may have indeed been dangerous for the faith, but not all of them were. It is just that they became heretical because certain people in power considered them to be outside orthodoxy.

So I ask now, "What are we so afraid of?" God is bigger than religion. The water I mentioned earlier can never be completely contained in the plumbing. I realized long ago that I was not called to be defender of the pipes but one who could help lead others to water.

I end this chapter by sharing again some of Weatherhead's original words. Writing this book is in part my way of honoring him for the help he gave me. His writing is the platform I am using to share some thoughts about the need for a "generous orthodoxy" today. Weatherhead quotes from Professor Henry Chadwick's Gifford Lectures:

> From earliest times it has been characteristic for Christian believers to 'confess' their faith in the form of credal or quasi-credal affirmation. The primary function of the affirmation was not so much to test the correctness of an individual's doctrinal beliefs as *to act as a pledge of loyalty and expression of confidence in God.* . . . Testing orthodoxy by creeds was a secondary function which came into prominence during the unhappy controversy of the fourth and fifth centuries; and by many important

8. Berger, *A Rumour of Angels,* ix.
9. Huxley, *T.H. Huxley on Education,* 29.

theologians of the time the process *was regarded as a most regrettable necessity.*"[Italics mine][10]

After quoting Chadwick, Weatherhead adds his own comment about administering tests of orthodoxy:

> Well as for me, I acknowledge no such necessity. Christ did not do so. He drew word pictures called parables with such winsome clarity that men, gazing upon them and meditating on them, could *SEE* the truth. No argument or logic carries the same degree of conviction as *insight*, and it is the kind of conviction by which we know that dawn over the Alps on a perfect morning is beautiful. Argument cannot produce it and doubt cannot remove it. The outward beauty meets the inward recognition and in our hearts we *know*.[11]

If you are or have been "dissatisfied or disillusioned," look up, brother or sister pilgrim, to that place where there is a new dawn, a whisper where the ruined house once stood, and drink of that water that is always ready to refresh and revive you. . . . Let's continue our journey.

10. Weatherhead, *The Christian Agnostic*, 33.
11. Ibid., 33.

2

I Believe; Help My Unbelief!

THERE IS A STORY in the ninth chapter of the Gospel of Mark where a desperate father is trying to get Jesus' attention in the midst of a crowd that is quickly becoming a mob.[1] This poor man has evidently tried every doctor and every clinic around to gain help for his son, who was unable to speak and experiencing seizures, which led people to believe that he was demon possessed.

Refraining for now from reinterpreting this scene of demon possession—an accepted element of the worldview of that time—into modern medical formulas, let's simply let the story be a story of faith seeking understanding. In the middle of this mob scene, the father pleads with Jesus for any help Jesus can give, "If you are able to do anything, have pity on us and help us!"

Jesus repeats the father's first few words, "If you are able!" and adds, "All things can be done for the one who believes." The way I interpret Jesus' response to the father reveals what might seem like a strange question, "If *you* are able—are *you* able to muster up some faith?" The man could have puffed out his chest and blustered, "You bet I can! Why, I'm willing to offer you a supersized affirmation right here on the spot. Just tell me what to say and I'll say it!"

But what the man does say rings down through the ages for any who are strugglers and wrestlers when it comes to the faith

1. Mark 9:14–29.

16

thing. In the midst of a moment of honesty, which may have stopped the world from turning for Jesus, the man shouts out, "I believe; help my unbelief!" I appreciate his honesty because it offers us a glimpse into the way Jesus responds to this cry from a father's heart. It is good news for this frightened father, and it is good news for us.

Jesus smiles as he hears this man proclaiming the truth of his experience in an affirmation of both belief and doubt. "So be it," thinks Jesus. (Okay, I admit that I am putting thoughts into Jesus' mind but, after all, the New Testament is a relatively short book, and a lot of what Jesus thinks does not get put into words, so it is up to those who seek to follow him to imagine what he might have been thinking. Have at it; I do it all the time.)

The boy is then healed with some words of Jesus that bear remembering. Hear his words from Mark 9:25: "You spirit that keeps this boy from speaking and hearing, I command you, come out of him, and never enter him again!" Could it be that Jesus is speaking not only on behalf of the helpless boy but also on behalf of the father, who had been carrying a heavy burden of not being able to admit that his faith had also been full of doubt?

Jesus frees both the child and the father. Both now are able to speak. The boy is freed from some kind of malady of the mind or body, and the father is freed and accepted by a Jesus who understands and accepts the father's complicated blend of belief and unbelief. I offer you, the reader, this invitation from Jesus. "Be free to proclaim your belief and your unbelief." Jesus does not need or expect us to be in a position of certainty and does not want us to be burdened with guilt about our experience of doubt.

I have told many a weary traveler on the road of faith that having doubts does not mean that they have missed a turn and are now off the mark. I often ask them if they realize just how much experiences of wilderness and exile are part of the biblical story. The feeling of being off the path and full of questions is, in fact, part of the journey.

Certainty can be a self-protective measure that blocks out feelings of insecurity and fear, but it can also prevent us from growing deeper and developing strong roots. As Ann Lamott once wrote in her book *Plan B: Further thoughts on faith*, [2] "The opposite of faith is not doubt, but certainty. Certainty is missing the point entirely. Faith includes noticing the mess, the emptiness and discomfort, and letting it be there until some light returns."

Certainty can be a way of not allowing yourself to probe too deeply about matters of faith for fear the ground will crumble and fall from under your feet. You may feel like you are on solid ground if you refrain from all questioning, but, as in the poem quoted in the previous chapter, "From the Place We Are Right," this ground can too easily become "trampled and hardened," the kind of soil in which nothing can flourish. Digging up the ground can allow a more passionate faith to grow.

There are many in the church that long to hear the good news that doubting does not disqualify people from being Christian but who are timid in the asking. Those who think they are no longer fit for church because of the doubts they have also need to hear the good news about the plow of doubt that can actually enrich the soil of our lives in which we seek to discover truth.

One issue for those who think they can no longer be comfortable with the faith of their childhood, or the faith that the church seems to offer, or even mandate, is that this inclusion of doubt as part of the faith journey is not made evident. We in the church usually look and act like we are so certain of what we proclaim, sing, and witness. To those who look through the crack in the door, we seem so sure of ourselves. They sense that they and their questions are not welcomed or accepted.

This is why we need to re-hear Weatherhead's invitation to welcome the agnostics. He says that to have within our fold those who are asking questions will make us all healthier. So perhaps on our church signs we need a byline below the listed times of our worship services that says something like, "Come share our belief *and* our unbelief." After all, they are both biblical.

The good news is straight from Jesus as he accepts the father's unbelief as a beginning confession. This good news first came to

2. Lamott, *Plan B*, 256.

my head when my heart was full of fear. The old expression that the longest journey is but eighteen inches from the head to the heart was true for me as a young seminarian whose mind was filled with new knowledge about God, philosophy, ethics, church history, and a myriad assortment of other ingredients that one gets in the course of a seminary education.

I knew for sure that there was no way I could graduate from this place of learning and stand before a group of people and proclaim much of anything. I was, I suppose, like that struggling father in the story; I was captured by the fear that I did not have enough belief. What I now know is that, in part, my fear was founded on the misguided principle that I needed to give people certainty, a certainty that I did not have at that time.

An encounter that gave me hope while I was at seminary was with the writings of a Dutch theologian by the name of Søren Kierkegaard. It was Kierkegaard who helped me see, even then, that sometimes doubt and belief go hand in hand.

One of his books, *Fear and Trembling*, is an examination of the figure of Abraham, whose story we may read in the book of Genesis. God has told Abraham that he is to be the father of "a multitude of nations."[3] Finally, his son, Isaac, the long-awaited child of promise, is born to him at the age of one hundred. Years go by, and Isaac grows to manhood, much beloved by his father. One day Abraham gets a message from God that Abraham should go with two young men to the top of a distant mountain in order to offer Isaac as a sacrifice.[4]

Abraham is caught in a dilemma. As he understands it, that same voice in the wind that asked him to leave everything and, in faith, go to a place of mystery and that promised to make him the father of nations is now telling him to take a knife to Isaac. Abraham ascends the mountain to make his offering to this strange God. We do not know what Abraham had in his mind as he is faced with this terrible predicament. Rationally, he may not have known how to interpret this turn of events. We might

3. Genesis 17:5.
4. Genesis 22:1–14.

imagine, however, that he had developed a great deal of trust in God over the years.

As they approach the place of sacrifice, Abraham tells the two young men, "the boy and I will go over there; we will worship, and then *we* will come back to you.[Italics mine]"[5] It seems that Abraham was somehow convinced that God would find a way to keep his overarching promise and spare Isaac. He was willing to obey God because he had utter confidence in God and God's promises. With fear and trembling, he took the leap of faith, and it is because he did that we gained more insight into the nature of God—that God does not require, or appreciate, human sacrifice, which was a step forward in the ethics of that time.

Abraham is caught in what Kierkegaard calls the paradox of faith. Sometimes things do not seem to make sense humanly speaking, but there is a higher logic that the mind cannot grasp, but about which there is some deep inner conviction. We need the interplay of both our hearts and minds.

Kierkegaard says something profound about this paradox in his *Philosophical Fragments*:

> One should not think slightingly of the paradoxical; for the paradox is the source of the thinker's passion, and the thinker without a paradox is like a lover without feeling: a paltry mediocrity. The supreme paradox of all thought is to attempt to discover something that thought cannot think.[6]

Another interesting thing about Abraham is that while he is portrayed as a giant of faith in the Scriptures, he is also shown as someone who does not hesitate to wrestle with God with questions and arguments. Earlier in Genesis, Abraham is seen to be debating with God about the issue of God's justice in his dealings with the people of Sodom.[7] It was because Abraham had cultivated a relationship with God that he had certain expectations about

5. Genesis 22:5.
6. Kierkegaard, *Philosophical Fragments*, 46.
7. Genesis 18:16–19.

God's character and was able to contradict a view of God that did not hold up. In other words, he could recognize and call out the "bogy" that was not for him the true God. It was a measure of his faith and confidence in God that he could do this.[8]

So for Abraham, and often for us, belief and doubt form a kind of paradox. Both are happening at the same time; together they can create great passion, and energy. As you read this, I hope this allows you to take a deep breath and feel that your questions are not something to be denied but are a part of the journey of faith. As the poet Rainer Maria Rilke puts it, "Be patient towards all that is unresolved in your heart and try to love *the questions themselves*."[9]

The image I take away from this encounter with this old theologian, Kierkegaard, is a modern one. It is of a nuclear reactor where two elements are brought together. Nothing happens while the two elements are steady and balanced. But when they collide, great power is created. Belief and doubt are the makings of power. They do not have to be kept so separate and in reality can offer light for the journey. Remember, however, that the reaction may occur in the dark. We do not have to fear the darkness as much as we often do; it is often the place of great insight and learning.

Weatherhead quotes the Rev. Dr. W. R. Matthews, former Dean of St. Paul's, who said, "The mistake that 'orthodox' people make is to suppose that they have all the truth and that nothing more can be known."[10] Our inheritance from the modern age of rationalism has created an atmosphere where the rational and scientific are valued above all. Our task could be to admit with humility that there may be more to know than our minds can fathom. As Kierkegaard noted, "It is the duty of the human understanding to understand that there are things which it cannot understand, and what those things are."[11]

8. Rees, *Wrestling with Doubt, 170.*

9. Rilke, *Letters to a Young Poet,* 25.

10. Weatherhead, *The Christian Agnostic,* 36.

11. Kierkegaard, *The Soul of Kierkegaard,* 117.

In those days of my confusion while in seminary, Kierkegaard helped me make that journey from the head to the heart. He helped me realize that my questions were not something to be ashamed of but could be fuel for that reactor that was my mind and heart. We in the church can be caught between two extremes: the certainty of a handed-down faith that brooks no questioning, and on the other hand, the extremism of a world-view that discounts everything that cannot be scientifically proven. Somewhere in the midst of these two is a place for the mythic and the poetic and for a relationship of trust in God.

In the next chapters we will begin to reexamine some of the specific beliefs of the Christian faith. As we do this, we should keep in mind some more of Kierkegaard's words: "The truth is a snare. You cannot have it without being caught. You cannot have the truth in such a way that you catch it, but only in such a way that it catches you."[12]

So, if you have ever felt that your doubts about faith have gotten you tangled up in some sort of snare, take heart. We will, in this book, endeavor to love the questions and know that as doubts dig up the soil of our faith, we shall be caught up instead by a truth that is even larger than our own understanding.

12. Kierkegaard, *The Last Years*, 133.

3

How Do I Know What I Know?
Why Should I Believe?

The Question of Authority

As I am sharing these thoughts with you, I am rereading Weatherhead's words. His book was first published in 1965, the year I graduated from High School, yet to me it is timeless. Think of all that has happened since Weatherhead put ink to paper—just that phrase ought to tell you something. I imagine this scholar and pastor sitting in an office somewhere pounding away on an old typewriter. He did not even have an IBM Selectric. As you read this, do you even know what an IBM Selectric is? That is my point.

Weatherhead did not have spell check, nor could he use *Google* in order to do his research. The many writers, poets, and early church scholars he quoted came from primary sources, probably from books stacked up beside that old typewriter. He did not use his smartphone to text his friend to see if he could use a personal story about that time he helped him in the midst of a crisis of faith. He had to walk down the block to ask him personally because Weatherhead believed that true knowledge and authority is personal.

His words are still personal to me. They are like a breath of fresh air. They still live for me, and that is one reason I am writing this book. I want them to live for you.

In this chapter we are exploring questions related to authority. I started this book with the image of drinking the Kool-Aid. In his chapter titled "Authority and Certainty," Weatherhead discusses the issue that became critical for me at that crucial time of my life. The question I was wrestling with was "How can I swallow all this and then claim it as truth if, in my heart, I feel like it is not yet true for me?"

You can imagine the possible answers to this question: I should believe certain things just because the Bible tells me so, or the preacher says it is so, or the church teaches it, or my mom and dad have said it, and so on. How many people have I spent time with over these forty years of ministry who, in one form or another, speak words to me that say something like, "I know I'm supposed to believe all this and that I'm not supposed to question . . . (fill in the blank: God, the Bible, the church, the leader etc.) . . . *but* . . . "

To all this "you have to believe it because . . ." kind of thinking, Weatherhead responds that while a truth may well be an absolute truth, it will only be authoritative for us if we ourselves perceive it as true:

> In matters of religion I hold the view that authority lies only in the perception of truth by the individual, a perception which is not a matter of facts or arguments thrust on the mind from without, but is the mind's intuitive recognition of those facts as true, an activity of the mind from within.[1]

As I reread Weatherhead's words, I am tempted to simply stop and tell you to go find a now out-of-print copy of *The Christian Agnostic* and read it. But then I would not be taking my mentor's words to heart. For I think he would encourage me to listen to him but then to define truth for myself, and in turn, I encourage you to do that for yourself. I shall continue writing then, in hopes that, as his words of encouragement allowed me to keep seeking truth in experience, so they will help you embrace what Kierkegaard once

---

1. Weatherhead, *The Christian Agnostic*, 51.

wrote: "the crucial thing is to find a truth which is truth for [you], to find the idea for which [you are] willing to live and die."[2]

On the other hand, I am also aware of something that was true in Weatherhead's own time and that is perhaps even more relevant today. There is a danger, in our "what's in it for me?" culture, that relying on this kind of experienced truth can rapidly decay into radical subjectivism: whatever I think and feel is true; if it feels right, do it; if it feels good, try it. This kind of subjectivism can erode a very much-needed sense of community that is often lacking in American culture, where we seem constantly vigilant that someone is going to infringe on "my rights." It is important then to be part of a community where we can share our ideas and have others point out to us ways in which our beliefs may be purely self-serving.

John Wesley, the founder of Methodism, has been credited with positing four ways of examining our beliefs. According to the *Book of Discipline of the United Methodist Church*, "Wesley believed that the living core of the Christian faith was revealed in Scripture, illumined by tradition, vivified in personal experience, and confirmed by reason."[3] In other words, we should be diligent in our study of the Bible, be tuned into the historic and evolving teachings of tradition, and make sure that whatever we believe makes sense to us, both in terms of experience and reason.

In his chapter about authority, Weatherhead tells the famous story of an experience John Wesley had while traveling. He met a group of Moravians who possessed a depth of experience with God that Wesley did not have, despite his sound theological training. When he returned to Aldersgate Street, his heart was "strangely warmed"; at that moment "the inner authority based on experience and the outer authority of the church met"; he experienced truth for himself in such a vivid way that it captured him.[4]

Subjectivism can be a real danger, but the other extreme often leads to stagnation and even alienation for the true spiritual seeker who longs to *know* truth. In a Christian faith that often seems to

2. Kierkegaard, *The Essential Kierkegaard*, 8.
3. The United Methodist Church, *The Book of Discipline*, 80.
4. Weatherhead, *The Christian Agnostic*, 60.

limit that search or even disdain it, we also need to hear this invitation to seek after a truth that resonates with us.

I remember a young woman who was a member of one of my churches. She was troubled by the various creeds of the Christian faith and frustrated by many of the traditional beliefs. She disappeared for a couple of years and then one day walked through the door of my office. Slamming the door behind her, she marched up to where I was sitting at my desk and almost screamed, "Why in the hell am I back here?" She then told me about her various pilgrimages to find truth. She had tried Hare Krishna, a bit of Judaism, a taste of Buddhism, a touch of Wicca, followed by a period of nothing. "Why did I come back here last Sunday?" she asked.

I listened to some more of her odyssey, and then responded simply, "Linda, I think you are searching for a defining story. Even though you have trouble with some of this Christian faith, what you need to hear is that what the Jesus thing is really all about is that it offers a story that can shape your life." At some level, she had been grasped by the defining story—that is why she had come back—but she needed to hear the story from a different perspective.

We all need a defining story, and the Christian story is a very powerful one with its themes of covenant and community, grace and goodness, exodus and exile, suffering and resurrection. In olden times, communities used to have a shared narrative that held the community together and that gave shape and meaning to the lives of individuals. In modern times, the shared narrative has largely disintegrated, and people have for the most part been left alienated, cut adrift from a defining story.[5]

The Christian faith, rather than being tossed aside as something antiquated and useless, needs to be re-imagined, re-stated, in order to provide the same sustenance that it once did. It contains much of value that can lead people to the source of the living waters. It is good to appreciate the wisdom and insight that religions that are not your own can bring to the table, but if you are

5. Hollis, *Tracking the Gods*, 26.

constantly digging shallow wells in many places, you cannot reach the depths that you can by digging one well in one place.

By digging deep into Christianity, reading the Bible with imagination and passion, and taking the time to learn as much as you can about it, both on your own and in community, it will slowly shape and transform you. Spend time in contemplation and service, seeking the Christ you have met in the pages of Scripture, and you will find that you have become part of this beautiful story, and you will resonate more and more with its deepest truths.

Since I referred to Linda's journey as a kind of odyssey, let me lift up an image that can counter the temptation to stand in isolation as our own beacon of truth. Because of our own pre-conceived notions, desires, and prejudices, we sometimes want to shape God in our image rather than the other way round. We need something to bind ourselves to that will guard against this.

The image comes from the original Odyssey, one of the two great epic poems attributed to the ancient Greek writer, Homer. The hero of the poem, Odysseus, sailing homeward, must pass the island of the Sirens. Sirens were beautiful women whose alluring voices tempted many sailors to follow their seductive singing only to end up shipwrecked on the rocks that surround the island.

In order to be able to sail past the island, Odysseus orders his men to plug their ears with beeswax. He knows that if they heard the beguiling voices, they would not be strong enough to resist the temptation. However, because he wants to be able to hear the beautiful singing himself, he orders the men to tie him to the mast of the ship and not to change course under any circumstances, even if he were to break free from his chains.

In other words, he is not putting his whole trust in his own powers and ability to discern the truth. Rather, he has freely decided to bind himself to something. As they pass the island, he discovers the wisdom of his binding. His screams to his men to unbind him go unheard. The beeswax in their ears prevents them from hearing both the Sirens' voices and Odysseus' commands.

Sometimes we need to bind ourselves to the essence of the defining Christian story so that the demands of our self-interest, what some call our false self, do not lead us astray. Being bound to this story can sometimes be difficult but at the same time it can give us a freedom unlike any other. I often tell young people who are hell-bent on discovering the alluring island called "freedom" that there is no such thing as freedom. We are always bound to something. Our only choice is to decide what we shall bind ourselves to.

In terms of religious truth, you may not have been coerced exactly, or dragged kicking and screaming to the altar in order to make some kind of profession of faith, but your parents, your clergy, or your peers may have put some pressure on you. Perhaps it was the thing to do, so you did it. Perhaps now you wish to cast aside those vows that were not truly yours in the first place. That may be the right thing to do, but I suggest that you not throw the baby out with the bathwater. There may be many aspects of what you have learned that can go, but some may just need more light. Weatherhead's suggestion to put the aspects of faith that make no sense to you in a drawer awaiting further light is a good one. In a new light, those old, tired tenets of faith might take on a different shape.

That pilgrim woman who slammed the door of my office wanted her freedom to sail toward whatever island she deemed worthy but discovered that her freedom did not give her what her heart longed for. I offered her a second chance to look at that "old, old story of Jesus and his love"[6] to see if she could find a make a new home in that defining story. She took that second chance and came to the place where she had started and knew it for the first time.

So consider this a time for you to take a fresh look at the Christian faith. You may have been dunked beneath the waters of a baptismal pool or confirmed in the midst of doting parents, or maybe you simply drank the Kool-Aid. Perhaps you have said "no" to the faith of your past, or have never said "yes" to it. Whatever the case, I now offer you a chance to look again at the faith in the clear light of day and decide whether or not you wish to be part of that story.

Weatherhead reminds us that the word "religion" comes from the Latin word "re-ligare," which means to bind, or to link. He says

6. Hankey, "I love to tell the story," *The United Methodist Hymnal*, 156.

that true religion is a love affair, a "ligament between the soul and God," not a list of beliefs. *"The authority, then, in religion, is my inner response to the religious truth put before me."*[7]

Another of my mentors is Richard Rohr, a Franciscan friar who is an internationally known writer, speaker and founder of the Center for Action and Contemplation in Albuquerque, New Mexico. In his book, *"Falling Upward: A Spirituality for the Two Halves of Life,"* he writes about the true task of religion:

> It is religion's job to teach us and guide us on this discovery of our True Self [which he has defined elsewhere as the mysterious interweaving of human soul with God[8]], but it usually makes the mistake of turning this into a worthiness contest of some sort, a private performance, or some kind of religious achievement on our part, through our belonging to the right group, practicing the right rituals, or believing the right things. These are just tugboats to get you away from the shore and out into the right sea; they are the oars to get you working and engaged with the Mystery. But never confuse these instruments with your profound "ability to share in the divine nature" itself (2 Peter 1:4).[9]

Rohr differentiates between the pipes and the living water of God, going back to our metaphor from chapter 1, saying that religion is helpful to get us engaged with the mystery but that we should never forget that we have the living water of God within us. He believes that it is perhaps easier for us to understand the true role of religion in the more spacious second half of life, when, hopefully, we have transcended the attempt to define ourselves by differentiating ourselves, when we realize that we are part of the wide community of humankind, that we are "all in this together." He writes that those in the second stage of life:

> are able to "contain" more and more truth, more and more neighbors, more and broader vision, more and

7. Weatherhead, *The Christian Agnostic*, 55.

8. Rohr, *Immortal Diamond*, 1–26.

9. Rohr, *Falling upward*, 98.

more of a mysterious and outpouring God. Their God is no longer small, punitive, or tribal. They once worshiped their raft; now they love the shore where it has taken them. They once defined signposts; now they have arrived where the signs pointed. They now enjoy the moon itself instead of fighting over whose finger points to it most accurately, quickly, or definitively.[10]

Ah, what freeing and refreshing words for spiritual pilgrims who are looking for a more spacious faith. We can move beyond the fear that causes many to cling to the raft and the signposts and enter into the presence of the "mysterious and outpouring God." As we go out into that sea where we seek truth, Weatherhead has offered some words of wisdom that I have found liberating in my ministry as I have shared my faith with my congregation. Perhaps Weatherhead's words will help you:

> Christianity is a way of life, not a system of theological doctrines which must be "believed." ... [While] we must not thrust beliefs on people, belaboring their minds to try to make them accept orthodoxy, we may set these same beliefs before people, showing them the rich truth which we have found and which they may come to receive as their questing mind develops and grows. We say, in effect, not, "You *must* believe this and this," but "Here is the body of Christian doctrine which you may believe as your mind contemplates it." We want them to *see* and then they will believe.[11]

It is my hope that you, my sister and brother pilgrim, will take the chance to see for yourself the rich truths of the Christian faith, perhaps for the first time, in the pages ahead. As I continue to follow Weatherhead's outline of the major doctrines of the faith as he has ordered them in *The Christian Agnostic*, I will be using some of his thoughts and combining them with some of the new truths that I have found on my journey.

10. Ibid., 120–121.
11. Weatherhead, *The Christian Agnostic*, 61.

4

God

Do Pay Attention to the "Man behind the Curtain"

GOD. AS I TYPED that word on my computer, my cursor pulsed on and off beside it. Try it for yourself. You will see something that resembles the blinking of a monitor, like one that might be attached to someone you love as they lie in a hospital bed. You are sitting beside them, holding their hand, maybe whispering a silent prayer. People are known to pray in this situation even if they say they do not believe in the word that appears beside the cursor's pulse. I am not the first person to say that if there were no God, we would need to make one up.

Freud said that we invented the idea of God to fulfill a need for some cosmic parent figure that we can talk to, blame, or beg from. There may be some element of truth in Freud's words, but, sorry Sigmund, your saying that does not mean that there really is not a "man behind the curtain." Anyone who does not know what I am talking about with this man behind the curtain image has been living under a rock too long. It comes, of course, from that famous scene in the movie based on L. Frank Baum's book, in which Dorothy and her pilgrim companions, the Tin Man, the Scarecrow, and the Lion who longs to be brave finally have their audience with the grand and glorious Wizard of Oz.

As they approach the wizard in the great hall of Oz, they see eruptions of flames and smoke, and then a terrible projected face appears behind the flames. A commanding voice shouts admonitions to the frightened seekers after truth and freedom, "I am Oz, the Great and Powerful. How dare you approach me?" As Dorothy and her friends, meekly, and with fear and trembling, attempt to make their requests to the apparently omniscient wizard, the booming voice, despite assuring them of his beneficence, belittles and insults the insignificant beggars and finally tells them to go away.

I could stop right here and tell you that some of the people who have come to me over the years seeking truth in the midst of confusion have an image of God much like the one in this scary scene. For them, God is some distant voice behind a curtain that makes them feel small and insignificant, or guilty and afraid. Some of them have listened to that voice and have indeed gone away.

Ah, but let's continue to the famous scene in which Dorothy's little dog, Toto, becomes the whistle blower. He runs up to the curtain that is part of the mystical array of the great Oz and then, grabbing hold of the bottom of it, pulls it aside to reveal . . . nothing more than a man speaking into a microphone. The man is frantically pulling on all kinds of wheels and levers to create the magnificent illusion that the whole land believed to be the Great Wizard of Oz.

The "wizard," exposed, tries to pull the curtain back around himself and, as a last-ditch effort to maintain the illusion, shouts even louder into the microphone, "Pay no attention to the man behind the curtain!" This flim-flam would-be wizard was hoping to sustain the mystery that was concealing a lie, but Dorothy would have none of it. She protested this bulldoggery and demanded that the real wizard please stand up.

What Dorothy needed was a real and powerful wizard and she was determined that no mere illusionist behind a veil would stop her from completing her vision quest and championing the needs of her companions; they also had dreams they wished to come true and knew that they needed outside help to gain inside fulfillment.

This sounds to some people a lot like the whole "God" thing, does it not? Have you ever thought that the God you were told about who was supposed to be all powerful and all knowing has been revealed to be no more than an illusion of smoke, fire and levers?

As we read on in the Wizard of Oz story, however, we come to realize that there was in fact *something more than just a man* behind the curtain. We discover, as the story unfolds, that although the old man was indeed part of an illusion, he was only representative of what could be. He helped Dorothy and her companions realize that what they were looking for was already within them. The seekers already had everything they needed; they just did not know it.

The wizard gave them a hand up on inner knowledge and potential. Each of them was already in possession of gifts that were hidden behind feelings of powerlessness and insignificance. So what did the wizard do? He blessed them for who they already were. The results? A mind of wisdom, a heart full of caring, and a breast filled with courage—and, of course, a way home.

No wonder children of all ages love this story. It could be an appendix in the Bible for the benefit of those who will listen and pay attention. God is already within you and always has been; it is God who blesses you and fills you with wisdom, love and courage. In God, you are already at home.

So many people through the ages have thought that the idea of God is a made-up concept, that there is no real God behind the curtain. They take a strange joy in taking on the role of Toto, the philosophical whistle blower, attempting to expose God as just an illusion, or a delusion. However, many scientists today are recognizing that perhaps there is something more behind the curtain than they had thought. As a teaser, I will tell you that I am going to end this chapter with the words not of a theologian but of a physicist who has something to say about this "man behind the curtain."

For now though, let's go back to where we began this chapter, with the word "God" beside a blinking cursor. Yes, the word "God" is but a word. Some of us act like we have "got" God just because we can type these three little letters that appear on the screen or speak the word out loud. Wrong. In fact, this one little word represents a very big concept, and with it we will begin our own vision quest.

The Hebrew people knew better than to think they had "got" God. In the Hebrew Scriptures, the word "God" is so full of mystery that it cannot be written or spoken. When the sacred name is used, a different word is respectfully substituted, usually *Adonai*, which is often translated "LORD." It is interesting to note that because of the layered literary and theological traditions that make up the Scriptures, many different titles are used for God, including *Yahweh*, *Elohim*, and *El Shaddai*. The one behind the curtain has many names and has been elusive from the beginning.

By the way, if you think I am just reaching into old movie archives in order to come up with this curtain image, you can also find it in the Hebrew Bible. In Exodus 26:31–34, describing the specifications for the Temple, the text says that there should be a curtain separating "the holy place from the most holy place." They believed that it was behind the curtain, in the most holy place, that God resided.

To help me say something about this "man" behind the curtain, I want to share my favorite Bible story, which you can read in Exodus 33. Moses is attempting to get God to come out from behind "the curtain" to reveal his face.

First though, I will give you a little background to this story. Just before this bargaining scene, Moses discovers his band of former slaves— the very people he has only just led out of slavery from Egypt—having a kind of rock concert, complete with mosh pit. It seems the people are growing tired of waiting on both Moses and God. While Moses is up the mountain, meeting with God within a dense cloud, the people gather together all the loot they have stolen from their former slave owners, melt it down, and shape it into a golden calf.

I mentioned earlier that it seems that if people do not have a God, they will make one. Here is a case in point. In this story, the so-called people of God turn into a mob and take things into their own hands. This is a preview for what a coming attraction called the church is capable of doing if people are left to their own devices. But that is for later.

Moses comes down from the mountain and crashes the party. He is so mad and disappointed by the actions of the people that he throws the book at them. Well, I am getting ahead of myself, there were no books yet, but he does throw the stone tablets that have the original Ten Commandments carved on them. They break into pieces. Now you know the first time the Ten Commandments were broken.

So, getting back to my favorite story, we again see Moses talking with God.[1] He dearly wants God to step out from behind the curtain. He is getting impatient with how things are going. Moses asks God, "So, what's the plan? Show me the purpose in all this." In the old language of the day, Moses wants to "see God's face."

As you are reading this, if you have ever wanted to understand just why things happen as they do and what God's role in it all is, well, that is nothing new. Moses wants the same thing. He figures that if he is going to be in God's employment, he needs to know the CEO's five-year plan. However, Moses, like the rest of us, does not get exactly what he wants when it comes to understanding God's ways.

In response to Moses' request, God makes a deal with Moses. God tells Moses that yes, God's presence will be with Moses and the people and that God will give them rest, but when it comes to being allowed to step behind the curtain to see God's face—that is just not going to happen. God tells Moses to stand in a crevice on the side of the mountain while God's glory passes by in a kind of parade, but the only thing that Moses will be allowed to glimpse is God's "backside." You can translate that in whatever way is best for you.

If you want to be crass, and you are not feeling very spiritual, you can say God shows his "ass." It is biblical after all. (Later in the book, I will talk about how the phrase "it is biblical" is greatly misused.) If you think I am being irreverent in using this word—even though that is what many scholars say may be the most accurate

1. Exodus 33:12–23.

translation of this Hebrew word—then I can clean it up by translating it as God turns his back on Moses. Does that sound any better? The truth is we are not going to like this no matter how we translate it. We want to *know*, especially in our day when we are accustomed to being able to find out answers to so many of our questions. People in ancient days lived in the midst of mystery much of the time. They did not know about galaxies and quantum physics. They figured the stars hung from a dome in the sky, and the intricacies of the way things worked were left to spirits of the air.

Moses' entreaty to God to show his face is a precursor to the plea of my hero from the Gospel of Mark, "I believe; help my unbelief!" However, we are dealing with the real God here, not the one we would like God to be, nor the one we shape from our disappointments. The real God, remember, is full of mystery. The real God often remains hidden from us because this hidden mystery is a part of who God is, but as we shall see, it is not all that God is.

As I listen to people who are having trouble with God, I recognize that what they are really struggling with is their concept of God—which has been formed by piling together everything they have been given from the past and then shaping it into a kind of "image." Yes, that does sound just like a golden calf, except without the party. But that is my point.

The old creation story says that God shapes people in God's image, not the other way around, but we do it anyway because it is human nature to do so. Nonetheless, the result of such shaping is not God; God is way bigger than our small images, and God is not so malleable as to be shaped into the various bumper sticker images that can become our user-friendly theology: "God is my co-pilot"; "Need a marriage counselor? Try me, signed God"; "God always answers knee mail." These ready-made images are formed because we long to "know." We really do want the "man" to step from behind the curtain.

It is probably time, or past time, that I step out from behind the curtain and admit that I often use the masculine pronoun for God because, well, it comes naturally to me since I am one of the guys, and it is biblical, after all. Okay, but now it is time to step up to the plate and confess that the real God, of course, is not male.

For sure, it is biblical to call God *he,* since the Bible was written and mostly edited by men at a time when men had the last word. But even in a heavily patriarchal culture, feminine images did sneak in—such as one of the names for God I mentioned earlier, *El Shaddai,* which can be translated "the breasted one"—and that is how it should be.

In today's world, many are careful to use inclusive language for God, recognizing that God is beyond gender. So I do often try to use the word *God* instead of *he,* but maybe I have been lazy up till now. Since we are on a journey, I will try to be more careful. The point is that the Bible is rich with many metaphors for God, and we need to remember that these do not define God; they just help us understand some things about the mystery we name God. God is bigger than gender and larger than all of our images.

J. B. Phillips wrote a book years ago entitled *Your God Is Too Small.* In this book he uncovers many of the labels we put on God. He points out that our understanding of God has for the most part remained static all the while our understanding in other areas of life has expanded. He tries to replace inadequate, and even destructive, concepts of who God is with some more constructive ideas.

In order to help people have some different ways of looking at who God is, I often introduce them to Process theology. Process theologians use words and images we don't usually associate with God. They describe God as vulnerable and limited, deeply affected by the suffering of creation, but unable to intervene in dramatic ways to set things right. This seems to run counter to operational ideas such as God's omnipotence and God's immutability.

For Process theologians, God does not stage-manage from outside or afar; God's power is from within. It is ever-present, life-giving, persuasive, and redemptive.[2] C. Robert Mesle believes that God does not intervene (in the ways we might wish) to prevent or alleviate suffering not because God is indifferent or because

2. Cobb, *The Process Perspective,* From the introduction by Jeanyne B. Slettom, 1.

God chooses not to, but because "freedom is an inherent feature of reality."[3] Without freedom, all the evolutionary processes that determine what we know as creation would not have been possible.

For Mesle, God's power lies in love and patience. God shares in the suffering of the world and has been working for billions of years, within and through all creation (of which we are a part) "to create something good out of what the world makes possible."[4]

> It is true that the God of process theism cannot wave a magic wand and end the suffering. Process theology is for those who have given up belief in a picture of God whose only virtue is unused power, or power used selectively for a lucky few. Instead, process theology calls us to accept a world in which we must bear responsibility. God can work in the world; but God can work in our world most effectively, most quickly, through us. . . . God's primary avenue to liberation is through responsive human hearts. We can wait for supernatural miracles or we can roll up our sleeves with God and get to work.[5]

For some people, to put God and vulnerability in the same sentence is simply too much. All I know is that the "all-powerful" God of my childhood is not big enough to handle real faith, nor the reality of the world in which we live. Instead of this "bogy that does not exist that [we] miscall God," we need the nail-torn Christus of Markham's poem, the Cosmic Christ (a title we'll be exploring soon), the suffering one who is the "hero of the battling universe."

Somehow it is partly through this suffering, and Jesus' identification with those who suffer, that healing and wholeness spring forth. This Jesus, in whom the whole fullness of God dwells,[6] who reveals to us the vulnerability of God, who voluntarily takes on suffering, and who calls us to participate in the healing of the world, will be the subject of the next chapter.

3. Mesle, *Process Theology*, 59.
4. Ibid., 62.
5. Ibid., 79.
6. Colossians 2:9.

In the bibliography, I have listed some introductory books on Process theology in case you might want to pull back the curtain to discover a God that might surprise you—or at least some concepts of God that might. At times it may seem that we are dealing with a mystery that we can never completely possess and even that this ultimate reality is turning a "backside" to us, but it is, and it has always been, God's desire to reach out to us. The witness of the Bible is that God is constantly yearning for God's people and that God shows up in the most unexpected and surprising ways.

We can be duped by a culture of instant technology that produces a growing impatience with wonder, mystery and awe. If we are not careful, we become quickly disappointed with a God who does not show up in the way we expect. Ask Job about this God. In the Hebrew Bible, Job finally realizes, after a number of chapters in the book that bears his name, that the real God is not the man behind the curtain nor any kind of wizard.

Job discovers that the real God answers the "Why don't you show me your ways?" question with another question. God says to Job, "Hey, I'll step from behind the mystery and let you understand me if you will first answer my questions." Job says "Bring it on!"[7]

If you want to read the exact answer, you can find it in the book of Job, but for now, a paraphrase will do. God more or less says to Job, "Where were you when I created those galaxies that you have not even discovered yet? Where were you when I carved out the Grand Canyon with my little finger? Where were you when I thought up the butterfly? Where were you when I shouted to the ocean: 'Stop here because I would like to have some beach now!'?"

In other words, God says to Job: "How do you think you are really going to understand all that I am? Go read your Bible, and remember what I said to Moses. When it comes to the real God, you only get a glimpse. But it is not the golden calf; it is the real me with all the mystery, but hey, it is the *real* me, and I do know your name because I made you in infinite mystery. Go read a few Psalms to find out more—and by the way—I love you. If this sounds harsh to you Job, remember I am reaching out to you

7. Job 38–42.

from the mystery. I choose to have a relationship with you. Keep looking for the glimpses."

I have been using stories from the Hebrew Bible to hold up for us the otherness of God because as we approach the New Testament we encounter almost a reversal. The Christian Scriptures offer us a unique revelation of the mysterious God into human existence. Weatherhead ends his chapter about God (called "God and Our Guesses") with some words about the evidence of God presented by Jesus, which are very insightful:

> On the lowest level of assessment Jesus Christ was the greatest religious genius the world has ever known. Suppose that imaginatively we said to him: "When you were nailed on the Cross and said, 'Father, into Thy hands I commit my spirit,' you were quite wrong. There was no one there. You only wished you had a father. I know better than you. There isn't a God." Would it not be rather like telling Beethoven that he could not write music, Shakespeare that he was no artist, and Einstein that he had got his sums wrong?[8]

Before I end this chapter though, I will leave you with what I promised: some physics and a bit more. Firstly, here is the bit more—some thoughts about God (which actually relate to the physics) from two eminent theologians of the last century, Rudolf Otto and Paul Tillich.

For Rudolf Otto, God is "the numinous," "the wholly other," or "the Holy Other." He says that an encounter with this God invokes *mysterium tremendum*, "a sense of awe-filled mystery, characterized by astonishment and humility."[9] According to Otto, an encounter with the numinous is a primal element of human experience. Further, "the mystical experience of something more, of a transcendent Holy Other, is . . . characterized by a deep sense of connectedness and unity."[10] Paul Tillich called God, "the ground of all being,"—"the power of being in everything and above

8. Weatherhead, *The Christian Agnostic*, 90.
9. Jacobs, *Religion and the Critical Mind*, 176.
10. Ibid.

everything, the infinite power of being . . . the cause of finite beings, and their substance."[11]

Quantum physics endeavors to describe the behavior of matter and energy at the most microscopic of levels. Scientists have
discovered that there is a moving reality below what can be seen
that provides the substance and energy of all that is. So here is what
could be called "the ground of all being," even if you profess to be
an atheist, and perhaps the only choice really is whether or not to
relate to this ground of all being with a sense of wonder and awe.

Physics as well as theology can be a doorway to experiencing some of this wonder that I believe to be God. As I write this,
scientists think they have discovered the mysterious Higgs boson
particle, sometimes termed in the popular media the "God Particle." This elusive particle is the missing link to what is known
as the "standard model"—what some consider a theory of almost
everything. There needs to be something that makes matter stick
together to form mass. Scientists think they have finally discovered this missing particle that binds reality together.[12]

In his book *The Language of God*, Francis Collins, current
director of the National Institutes of Health, and former longtime
head of the Human Genome Project, tells of his journey from unbelief to belief. Collins came to faith not because of any theological
construct but because of his work in both physics and biology.

In a chapter about the origins of the universe, Collins writes
about the Anthropic Principle. This principle states that there
are fifteen physical constants, for example, the speed of light, the
strength of nuclear forces, the force of gravity, and so on, that all
need to have specific values in order to result in a stable universe
capable of sustaining complex life forms. Collins believes that the
chance of this happening randomly is almost infinitesimal.[13] "For
those willing to consider a theistic perspective, the Anthropic

11. Tillich, *Tillich,* 165.
12. Caroll, *The Particle at the End of the Universe,* 11.
13. Collins, *The Language of God,* 74.

Principle," concludes Collins, "certainly provides an interesting argument in favor of a Creator."[14]

Another scientist, MIT-trained physicist, Gerald Schroeder, an Orthodox Jew and Bible scholar, wrote a book called *God According to God*, in which he combines his many years of scientific research and biblical study to present his view of God, which is a lot like that of the Process theologians. Schroeder points out in his first chapter that contrary to popular belief, God is not controlling every detail of what goes on,[15] and that it is in "this withdrawal of absolute Divine control [that] we discover the source of chance and choice within our world."[16] For Schroeder, the freedom that God gave both humans and Creation in general is essential to the way that the world operates.[17] He goes on to suppose that God experiences sorrow and regret about the consequences of that withdrawal.

In part, Schroeder, in his first chapter, does what I have been attempting to do in this chapter. So much information about God is misinformation, based on old ideas and even old science. Schroeder thinks that God has become reduced to what we can deal with, rather than being a dynamic God who can only be glimpsed by those who dare to bring both their belief and doubt to the edge of the curtain.

At the conclusion of his book, Schroeder quotes a fellow scientist and author, Michael Shermer, who does not believe in a supernatural view of the world: "We exist together for a narrow slice of time . . . , a passing moment on the proscenium of the cosmos."[18] Schroeder picks up on Shermer's inadvertent use of the word *proscenium*, which, as Schroeder explains, "is none other than the part of the stage in front of the curtain and the audience. Shermer hit the proverbial nail right on the head. We live our lives on the

14. Ibid., 78.

15. Schroeder, *God According to God*, 99.

16. Ibid., 104.

17. Schroeder, *The Science of God*, 170.

18. Ibid., 21.

proscenium, the visible part of the stage. But as every theatre devotee knows, the show is directed from *behind the curtain.*"[19]

So, there we have it. We are back to that place where we started—with the "man behind the curtain." I hope these words have helped you take a look, or at least a glimpse, at God again as if for the first time. When it comes to awe and mystery and the Holy Other and the ground of all being, there need to be many first times—over and over.

Now let's try a glimpse of one who is sometimes known as "the human face of God."

19. Ibid., 22.

5

The Story of the One Who Made
This Christian Agnostic Christian

Or

I Think It Must Have Been
a Different Jesus

WHEN I WAS SEVENTEEN, the rule was I could not date on a school night. I was allowed to go to church, however, and since there was a youth rally going on all week at a neighboring church, I figured out a way to take a date to the Thursday night event.

It started out as not such a hot date, nor was it in its beginning a very spiritual experience. It seems the girl I took with me had more interest in a friend of mine who was on the football team with me and who was sitting on the other side of her. She was flirting with him even as the preacher for the evening was giving a kind of invitation. The guy in the pulpit—and no, I do not remember his name even though what he was about to do changed my life—gave some rather strange instructions:

"Hold out your hands, and close your eyes, and ask Jesus to take your hands and lead you through life. I know this may sound silly or strange to you at this age, and it might be a bit embarrassing, but everyone will have their eyes closed, so it doesn't matter. Just do it for me."

Some words the preacher of the evening had said earlier that night had caused something to stir within me that I did not understand. I was confused because, after all, I was not there for religious reasons. It was simply an excuse to date this girl who now seemed to have other inclinations.

Then it happened. I felt something or someone touch my hands. I figured it was my date acting up because she sure was full of herself that night. I looked over to my left, hoping the preacher would not notice I had my eyes open, and there was my date and the guy with whom she had been flirting sitting there with their eyes closed and their hands held out.

It was then I think I experienced something like what the Bible refers to as "the fear of the Lord." In an instant, and it was an instant, my heart started pounding and I was afraid. I wondered what in God's name was happening and, by the way, that is a good way to put it. I tentatively looked out in front of me, and there were hands holding my hands.

That is about all I can say. I quickly closed my eyes. They were now filled with tears. I was embarrassed. I did not want to allow my date to see this supposedly tough guy with tears in his eyes. Then the preacher said something like, "If any of you want to come down to the altar tonight and ask Jesus to lead you through life, please come." I noticed that some other guys were going up there, so I figured I could conceal my tears by going up with the others.

When I got there and knelt, I whispered to whoever was listening, "Okay God, if that's how it's going to be, I'll give you me." The rest is history. I have been a United Methodist minister for these forty years.

Trust me, I came to doubt that "vision" of hands. I tried to run away from those hands. I tried to submerge the image of hands under doubt and layers of knowledge. I decided, through my study of the psychology of religion, that one could imagine such things. But I write these words to you because even though I am a Jacob—one who wrestles with God—and though I still have many questions, I no longer doubt that, whatever actually happened that date night long ago, I was captured by the mystical hands of a man named Jesus. He simply will not let me go even when I run away. I write these words to you, and I especially write this chapter about this Jesus, because of those hands.

I do not understand what happened that night. I believe that if you had been sitting on the other side of me, you could have opened your eyes that evening and you would have simply seen a teary-eyed adolescent with his hands held out in the air. Beside him, you would have seen his date, the woman who is now his wife of forty-five years, holding out her hands, and beside her would have been that friend of mine holding out his hands.

So, let me tell you about my Jesus. Sounds like some old gospel song does it not? And of course, the fact that I use the expression "my Jesus" is part of the problem for many people. Just who is the real Jesus? Brian McLaren describes in his book, *A New Kind of Christianity*, the many ways in which Jesus has been made and remade over the years and how our understanding of who Jesus is has developed.

McLaren begins by pointing out the evolution of people's perception of God throughout the span of the Hebrew Bible. The early texts were written in the context of a people accustomed to violence and tribal conflict in which lands were taken and whole groups of people were killed because they thought that God required it. By the time you get near the end of the narrative of the Hebrew Bible, however, God has become more a lover seeking out a mate than a conquering warrior seeking to establish a tribal kingdom.

In other words, it is the cultural and historical context of those who have described God that influences the way God is understood, and the same is true of our understanding of the identity of Jesus. McLaren writes that the early interpretation of the life and work of Jesus took place in the context of the Greek philosophical tradition, and within the economic, military and political atmosphere of the Roman Empire. This context produced the fall/salvation/heaven-or-hell narrative with which we are familiar.

Subsequent theologians have built up on this narrative to create the predominant picture of Jesus that we have today.

McLaren proposes an alternate vision of Jesus, one in which he emerges from within a story that has been unfolding throughout the whole of Jewish history, through the lives of those who preceded him, including Adam, Abraham, Moses, David, the prophets, and John the Baptist. When viewed this way, McLaren says that the Christian story highlights Jesus' announcement of a new way of life that is bigger than any religion. It emphasizes "God's faithful solidarity with all humanity in our suffering, oppression, and evil," and "God's compassion and call to be reconciled with God and with one another." This sounds a lot like the "nail-torn Christus," the "builder of roads," and "breaker of bars" of Markham's poem.

McLaren says this:

> So many people . . . have so utterly bought into the . . . black-and-white, soul-sorting Heaven-or-Hell Greco-Roman narrative that it has become the precritical lens through which they see everything, causing them to see some things that aren't there and rendering invisible many things that are. If they could only take off that set of glasses long enough to see Jesus in full color, in three dimensions, everything would look different. . . . .Thankfully, . . . more and more of us are discovering Jesus as Word and Lord colored outside the conventional lines. This Jesus, we discover, is far more wonderful, attractive, compelling, inspiring, and unbelievably believable than Jesus shrunk and trimmed to fit within them.[1]

You could say that Weatherhead took off that "set of glasses" that McLaren refers to. In his chapter about Jesus, he touches on many interesting questions about Jesus and sees Jesus in another light. He looks at doctrines such the virgin birth, Jesus' humanity and/or divinity, his miracles, the meaning of the Cross and his death, and the resurrection. I will address these issues, and perhaps a few more, in my own way.

---

1. McLaren, *A New Kind of Christianity*, 136.

First of all though, let me share with you one of my favorite songs written by a singer-songwriter friend of mine, Ed Kilbourne. His song, "A Different Jesus" reflects what McLaren and others in the progressive Christianity movement are trying to convey about Jesus and puts into words some of what I think and feel about "my Jesus."

The title of the song, its punch line (and one of the titles of this chapter), comes from the refrain of the song, which goes: "I said, 'I think it must have been a different Jesus, the one I met when I was just a child. / I thought I recognized the name, but the one I know could not have changed that much.'"

> A stranger stopped me and said, "Friend, do you know Jesus?"
> I surprised him when I said, "I'm sure I do."
> Then he handed me his Bible and told me where to look,
> and what to say, and how to pray to find the truth.
> But when I tried to talk, he wouldn't listen.
> When I wouldn't pray, he shook his head.
> So I gave him back his Bible, and I just hugged him.
> I don't think he understood a word I said.
>
> (Refrain)
>
> I was getting dressed for church on a Sunday morning,
> When a TV preacher used that name again.
> He shouted "Jesus! Jesus! Jesus!" as he danced across the platform.
> Pretty ladies in the front row said "Amen!"
>
> It was later on at my church when I remembered
> That the devil tempted Jesus with a show.
> If he'd just say the word, the world would watch him,
> But when Jesus said the word, the word was "No!"
>
> (Refrain)

Some will use his name to sell you books and records.
Some just use his name to curse and swear.
We've got bathroom Bible thumpers.

We've got these Jesus jingle bumpers.
People write his name most anywhere.
We've got politicians who pray to get elected.
People praise the Lord and carry guns.
How come the ones who use his name most often
Fail to recognize him when he comes?

Or they'd find he's always been the same old Jesus.
He hasn't changed in spite of what you've heard.
He's still a friend to sinners everywhere.

I never met a man who cared so much.[2]

The Jesus that Kilbourne sang about meeting as child is a different Jesus from the one that we often hear about from TV evangelists and others. The line in this song that seems to linger in the room is, "those who use his name most often fail to recognize him when he comes." So the question becomes, how do we recognize the real Jesus? Who exactly gets to lay claim to his *real* identity?

If you are interested, there are many books that reflect upon the different ways Jesus has been portrayed over the years, such as *American Jesus*, by Stephen Prothero, and *Saving Jesus from the Church*, by Robin Meyers. The book *The Illustrated Jesus through the Centuries*, by Jaroslav Pelikan, also gives a fascinating perspective on how each age has created Jesus in its own image.

Albert Schweitzer, who published his book *The Quest of the Historical Jesus* in 1906, asserted that those who claim to search for the real man in the midst of the woven garment that is the New Testament will not find what they are looking for. As Schweitzer explored the various efforts of those who searched for the

---

2. Kilbourne, "A Different Kind of Jesus," *The Best of Ed Kilbourne*. Track 11.

historical Jesus, he discovered that those doing the searching had each painted a picture of Jesus using their own colors.

Schweitzer concluded his book with these, perhaps familiar, words about Jesus:

> He comes to us as One unknown, without a name, as of old, by the lakeside, He came to those who knew him not. He speaks to us the same word: "Follow thou Me!" and sets us to the task which He has to fulfill for our time. He commands. And to those who obey Him, whether they be wise or simple, He will reveal Himself in the toils, the conflicts, the sufferings which they shall pass through in His fellowship, and as an ineffable mystery, they shall learn in their own experience Who He is.[3]

I suggest then that if we bring a Christian-skeptic kind of attitude, not only to the edge of that lakeshore, but also to the edge of the one who is that "ineffable mystery," and follow Jesus, as "One unknown, without a name,"—for it is perhaps in our naming him that we confine him—we can possess a more open and expansive view of Jesus than is often projected by those who "use his name most often."

In the book *A Heretic's Guide to Eternity*, Spencer Burke and Barry Taylor offer a view of Jesus that goes beyond Christianity and that looks at Jesus in the way that McLaren is suggesting—without all the accumulated ideas of later Christian thought. Burke and Taylor remind us that before the Council of Nicaea in 325 CE, there were many varieties of what would later be called Christianity. People believed many different things about Jesus, and it was not until later that certain followers of Jesus came to be labeled heretics. These people had all followed Jesus, much like Schweitzer suggests, through the toils, the conflicts, and the sufferings. They had followed him because they chose to follow him, not because it was the thing to do, nor in order to get the sweatshirt.

Doctrines such as those surrounding the virgin birth, the death of Jesus, or the Trinity were secondary in the lives of these followers to simply choosing to align their lives around Jesus' way.

---

3. Schweitzer. *The Quest of the Historical Jesus*, 403.

There was no intent to start a new religion. It was the Emperor Constantine who is credited, or blamed, for starting what we call Christendom, and some think that is when the trouble began. With the legitimization of Christianity, "right" belief or "orthodoxy" began to be important. Creeds were formulated to define the Christian faith; doctrines were either in or out. This also determined *who* was in and *who* was out. The biggest controversy in the creeds seemed to be centered on the nature and work of Jesus.

Those who ended up in the outside group are what I would call the minority report. They were labeled heretics, even though they still followed Jesus. Burke and Taylor quote the business guru Art Kleiner, who said that a heretic is "someone who sees a truth that contradicts the conventional wisdom of the institution—and remains loyal to both entities."[4]

Perhaps as you read this you realize that, at most, you are a heretic who is struggling to remain loyal to the church, or maybe you have decided that the institution called church is simply too small to contain your heretical thoughts about Jesus. Well hold on. Jesus is bigger than the institution that bears his name.

Burke and Taylor call for a Jesus who is bigger than the religion we call Christianity:

> The old order was not sufficient to contain Jesus' radical message, and that is just as true today . . . This tendency to hold on to the familiar remains a problem for many followers of God today. Religion becomes a place we retreat to, where we hear the old stories, lovingly preserved but frightfully disconnected from the realities of life. The rise of interest in fundamentalism is evidence of the desire for reassurance—for ways of fitting a complex world into manageable categories. But religions don't function at their highest and best when they attempt to provide simple answers to life's biggest questions . . . Undoubtedly some people will see this call to reposition questions of faith beyond religion as dangerous and unscriptural. Many who come from a religious point of view may be threatened by the challenge to consider Jesus beyond

4. Burke, *A Heretic's Guide to Eternity*, xxiv.

religion. But as [we] see it, religion finds its gravity in the light of the sun. It finds sustainability and life through its relationship to the sun.[5]

So step with me out into the sun, and let's take a look at Jesus. You know the drill by now, do you not? Let's again come to the place we started in our exploring and know it for the first time. It will be okay. Jesus can handle it. Many church folks cannot, but that is okay. Some of those church folks have probably ceased reading this by now. They figure I am a heretic in sheep's clothing, or to put it professionally, they might judge me to be a not-so-sure pastor in a shepherd's costume.

But remember, I am writing this book for you, since you are still reading it. Those other dear folks do not need to read this, because for them, faith may be equated with certainty. Let's just do what the Beatles sing, and "let it be."

Here is some "heresy" for you. Christ is bigger than Jesus. I think I first got this idea from Matthew Fox who, having been defrocked from the Catholic priesthood, is an official heretic. He speaks of the "Cosmic Christ," which I interpret to be the same Christus that appears in Edwin Markham's poem.

Matthew Fox writes in his book, *The Coming of the Cosmic Christ,* that "Christianity has been out of touch with its 'core,' its center, its mystical practice and cosmic awareness." He advocates reviving an ancient but forgotten doctrine, that of the Cosmic Christ, which he understands as the "'pattern that connects' all the atoms and galaxies of the universe, a pattern of divine love and justice that all creatures and all humans bear within them."[6]

This Christus was sort of crammed into the man Jesus, but the Christus is so much more than the earthly Jesus. I imagine that this is what John's Gospel calls "the Logos," or "the Word that became flesh and dwelt among us."[7] This Logos, according to the Scriptures, is the very power of God that was, and is, present in creation. This Logos is bigger than Jesus but is in Jesus. (If you think I am

5. Ibid., 20.

6. Fox, *The Coming of the Cosmic Christ,* 7.

7. John 1:14.

making this stuff up, look up something called "the pre-existence of the Logos." It is one of those doctrines that became enshrined in theology—and one you might want to put in a drawer awaiting further light—except that for now it might be useful to understand the whole Jesus thing.) The Christus, or the Logos of God, is kind of like "the Force" before Star Wars ever came up with the concept.

Since the Logos of God is pressed into the very flesh of Jesus, he ends up being quite a man. I like the way Process theology puts it: Jesus is divine because he is fully human. C. Robert Mesle, in his book *Process Theology: a Basic Introduction,* describes the difficulty that people often have in getting their heads around the claim that Jesus is both divine *and* human.[8] He says that if you see humanity and divinity as being two completely different "substances," that would mean that they are in two mutually exclusive categories. Consequently, to affirm that Jesus is a participant in both categories is a "logical absurdity."

He describes the response of Process theologian, John Cobb, Jr., to this problem. He says that the Process view does not see humanity and divinity as closed categories. They are a cumulative process of relational choices. The more we respond to God's call, the more God becomes incarnate in our lives. Jesus' life was lived fully responsive to God's call in such a way that he "became able to incarnate the Divine Logos in his life."[9]

Cobb goes on to say that "to be more loving is to be *both* more fully human *and* more fully divine. To be more relationally powerful, more capable of sharing the sufferings of others with healing love, is to be *both* more human *and* more divine."

If you listen carefully to people who "use his name most often,"—and I am using gasoline as a metaphor here—you can usually hear about either a low-octane Jesus or a high-octane Jesus. The high-octane Jesus comes off pretty much like an angel with a touch of humanity. The low-octane Jesus resembles a really good motivational speaker with a mix of the Pied Piper thrown in.

8. Mesle, *Process Theology*, 105, 106.
9. Ibid., 107.

So let's just say that Jesus is the God-man, or the Man-God, whichever way you want to look at the image. He is the human face of God. He is the best thing God ever did.

There is great story in the Gospels that portrays this. Jesus stands in line to be baptized by John. He takes a number and waits. In one of the Gospels, John has real trouble with this when Jesus' number comes up. John basically says, "What in God's name are you doing there standing in line like some regular guy? Remember who you are! You don't need this cleansing water. You are more than squeaky clean." (In other words, John is saying something like, "LeBron James does not need to sign up for basketball camp.")

Jesus responds to John with some words we need to hear, "Hush up, John. Even you don't really get who I am. I'm higher octane than some people can handle, and I'm a disappointing low octane to those who are expecting fireworks and magic—just baptize me for heaven's sake—get on with it."[10] This is obviously a loose translation of the text. I have extrapolated my paraphrase from the text, because, if you fast forward the story, you can see that Jesus is a disappointment, even to John, and he becomes a real threat to the religious leaders of the day.

So, let's go back now to the concept of the Cosmic Christ. Jesus, as a human being, contained as much as could be contained of Christus, but at the resurrection, all that Logos-stuff was released into the world; Jesus became loose and about. Neither the church nor the creeds can contain the Christus of God. So, why are some people so uptight about defining exactly who Jesus is? Rather than getting caught up in many arguments and definitions, the important thing is to have an experience of this Jesus who is loose and about in the world and to follow him. That is what changed my life and what can change yours.

As Robin Myers says in his book *Saving Jesus from the Church: How to Stop Worshiping Christ and Start Following Jesus*:

> The first step, however, must be a step backward. We have been traveling down the creedal road of Christendom since the fourth century, when a first-century spiritual

10. Matthew 3:13–14.

insurgency was seduced into marrying its original op-
pressor. Before there were bishops lounging at the table
of power, there were ordinary fishermen who forsook
ordinary lives to follow an itinerant sage down a path
that was not obvious, sensible, or safe. He might as well
have said, "Come die with me." . . . We have a sacred story
that has been stolen from us, and in our time the thief
passes for orthodoxy . . . Arguing over the metaphysics of
Christ only divides us. But agreeing to follow the essential teachings of Jesus could unite us. We could become
imitators, not believers.[11]

I give you also these words of encouragement from Meyers
as a way to make sure you know you are invited on this journey of
discovery about Jesus:

We know that before that fourth-century fork in the
road, there was but one road. The disciples called it "The
Way," and it was the only road that did *not* lead to Rome.
It took travelers into the heart of God, singing all the way.
It welcomed all who would come, especially the poor
and the lost, and the only trinity that mattered was to
remember where we came from, where we are going, and
to Whom we belong.[12]

Jesus welcomes all who will come. Weatherhead reminded
me of this long ago when I was lost amidst conflicting doctrines
and my disappointment with the institutional church. He helped
save my faith so that I could discover a Jesus who, yes, sometimes
needs saving from the church. That Jesus is alive and free. Let's
now look at some of the doctrines that can be speed bumps, or
even road blocks, to some pilgrims on the road of faith.

I drank the Kool-Aid as a young boy, so I assumed that because Jesus was divine, he could do anything; he was, after all, the
Son of God, born of the virgin Mary, who suffered under some
guy named Pontius and rose again to provide a really good, happy
ending to a story that actually made no sense to me at the time.

11. Meyers, *Saving Jesus from the Church*, 10.
12. Ibid.

Why did he have to be born to a virgin? Why did he *have* to die? And if God could do something as miraculous as resurrecting a dead corpse, why could God not come up with a more imaginative plan to spare the world than to have someone murdered in order to "save" me?

As a child when I asked some of the dispensers of the Kool-Aid why was it necessary for Jesus to die, they simply said, "He died for our sins." At least the virgin birth was a kind of magic trick, but the blood and death stuff simply did not make sense to me.

Let's take this in order. The text most often quoted to set up the idea of a virgin birth is Isaiah 7:14, from the Hebrew Bible, "Behold, a virgin shall conceive, and bear a son."[13] The Hebrew word that is translated as "virgin" actually means a "young woman"; it is a stretch to translate "young woman" as "virgin."

In actuality, the translation may not matter, because if the virgin birth happened as related in the Gospels of Matthew and Luke, it might just be a case of the writers looking for a proof text to back up the story. We preachers do it all the time. When we want to prove that something is "biblical," we seek out a certain text somewhere in the Bible to prove what we already know and believe. Sometimes, rather than doing exegesis, which is a careful examination of the text in its historical and literary context, we make the text fit our presuppositions, which is called "eisegesis."

In other words, we make the text fit the point we are trying to make. The biblical writers are known to do this, so there is precedent. This allusion to a virgin birth is an example. If in fact Mary conceived in a miraculous way by being overshadowed with the Holy Spirit, why not stretch an old text to set it up? The virgin birth is worth a little manipulation after all.

The modern-day question is "Did it really happen?" The only Gospels that mention a virgin birth are the Gospels of Matthew and Luke. The Gospel of Mark, which was written much earlier, in 70 CE, and which provided foundational material for the Gospels of Matthew and Luke, begins Jesus' story with his baptism by John. There is no mention of a virgin birth in the Gospel of John.

13. KJV Isaiah 7:14.

The first thing written after Jesus left was not a Gospel but a series of letters by a man named Saul who got knocked off his horse on the way to kill a bunch of Jewish heretics called Christians who were messing things up. Saul had taken it upon himself to rid the landscape of these intruders to the faith who were going around claiming that the long-awaited Jewish Messiah was a renegade itinerant preacher who was foolish enough to get himself crucified. This simply was not kosher and was bad for business, so Saul got certified by the powers that be to run a terror campaign against the bunch.

The only problem was that on the way to Damascus a funny thing happened. The very hero that the new heresy was championing showed up in a burst of light. This vision of Jesus scared Saul's horse so badly that he threw off his rider and, in a blinding moment, Saul the persecutor was converted to Paul the apostle by none other than the Commander-in-Chief of the rebels: Jesus himself.

Paul became as zealous about the new faith as he had been intent on stamping it out. He started churches all over the land but, wouldn't you know it, the folks in the new churches started bickering about exactly what the new faith was really about. So Paul had to write them a series of letters in an attempt to say what the real faith was and what it was not. Those letters are now the earliest writings we have in the New Testament.

All this rambling about the Saul-to-Paul character who became the first author of the faith and the original biblical theologian is to remind us that he did not mention any virgin birth either. So we have the earliest and latest Gospels and the earliest writings about Jesus all silent about a virgin birth. Strange, is it not?

So it seems that many have come to the Christian faith without needing to believe that Jesus was born of a virgin. This means you can too. One group of heretics from the first two centuries whom I hold in high regard were known as "adoptionists." It seems that they believed that Jesus was not born into his role as Son of God but that he was somehow adopted by God on the day he was baptized by John. Remember the words that came from the heavens that day? "This is my beloved Son in whom I am well pleased."[14]

In other words, they believed that Jesus was a really fine Jewish boy who truly paid attention to the teachings of the elders and to the leading of God in his life and who felt a stirring in him that he was supposed to not only *do* something special but *be* something special. Jesus ended up standing in line to be baptized, and when he came up out of the water, God called out something like, "You are the one I select to be my Messiah, my chosen one, my son."

If this kind of selection process bothers you, then believe in the virgin birth by all means. A lot of other people sure have. As we now know, it seems to have become one of *the* main things you are supposed to believe in order to wear the Christian sweatshirt. But, if for some reason a virgin birth is a speed bump for you, you can just take a slight left turn, miss the speed bump, and go right past the Kool-Aid stand. You will still be a Christian. A whole bunch of early Christians did that, and they followed Jesus all the same.

On a personal note, I can go either way on this one. I understand the scholarship that provides an alternative to a virgin birth, but I really like the story. Jesus does not have to be born of a virgin for him to be the Messiah, nor does he have to not have a biological father in order to be divine—for me. His special character and Messiahship is still a reality for me whether God adopted Jesus or somehow overwhelmed a young girl with more than she or anyone could imagine.

On the other hand, I really love the Joseph story. I once wrote a piece pretending I was Joseph. In my imagination, I pictured Joseph wanting so much to be with the young girl that he had become attracted to in Nazareth. Joseph's words were something like this:

> I had been in love with Mary for a long time and had rejoiced so gladly the day I asked her father for a betrothal contract and he accepted. So you can imagine how my heart was broken when she told me she was pregnant. I knew that the Law allowed me to take her to her father's

14. KJV Matthew 3:17.

door post and have the men of the village stone her to death for this abomination,[15] but I could not.

She was *my Mary*. Then came the dream—a sweaty wrestling match that I had with what seemed like an angel. I awoke and knew the fantasy she mentioned to me about a child that came from God was true. I did not care what people thought or believed. I would become an adoptive father, if God and Mary would have me. . . .

I love the story; I really do. It is more the story of a leap of faith than it is a magic trick of biology. The virgin birth ends up in the creeds so it sounds like it is a necessity, but before it is a requirement, it is a real love story. For me, it is the story of a man's love for a woman no matter what the situation. It is also a narrative about God's love for us all, whatever the family tree ends up looking like.

Weatherhead spends some time in his chapter on Jesus discussing how to understand, as best we can, the miracles of Jesus. There are times I almost wish Jesus had not been a miracle worker. It makes him so distant from us, and it leaves a lot of the people with whom I work as a pastor asking question like, "Why can't that happen today?" or "Where is *my* miracle?" Some of the nature miracles, like Jesus calming storms, changing water into wine, and some of his healings, can be interpreted as they were intended to be understood in John's Gospel, as indicators or signs that point to something bigger than the specific miracle.

For instance, calming seas became a sign of what the spirit of the risen Christ could do for an early Christian community whose boat was starting to rock and take in water. Feeding five thousand people with five loaves and two fish became not a magic trick but a sign that the risen Christ could take a bit of bread and a taste of wine and renew countless hungry and thirsty pilgrims.

Some of the miracles simply have to stand on their own. Scholarship tells us that whatever the real Jesus was, he was a healer and one who cast out "demons." Obviously, people back then believed in such a thing as demons. They did not have modern

15. Deuteronomy 22:20.

medicine and psychiatric principles. Whatever Jesus personally thought about the reality behind the understanding of "demons," his goal was to minister to people who needed healing, so, he drove out the demons in order to make them whole.

All I can tell you is that I use this image of demons all the time when I work with people who are dealing with addictions and other compulsive behaviors. I have asked many people in AA if they believe in demons and have gotten a real straight answer that they sure do.

Now for another doctrine that causes a lot of people to pause. It is often called the doctrine of the atonement. It is the one I alluded to earlier that was a real speed bump for me as a child. Why did Jesus have to die?

The short version of the answer is that his death was interpreted after the fact in the only way some of his followers could understand it. Imagine their original disappointment that the man they gave their whole lives to ended up beaten up and fried on a public electric chair. Afterwards, they experienced something we call the resurrection, but they still had to explain his death.

Like any good Bible-believing Christian, they dusted off a copy of the Scriptures and said something like, "By golly, here it is, right here. It says he would be wounded for our transgressions. By his stripes we are healed."[16] Then they gathered around the table for what used to be the highest point of their faith, the Passover meal, and they said, "Well, here it is again, except that Jesus has become the Passover lamb. His dying allows us to be free and forgiven."

In other words, they used Jewish sacrificial imagery to understand the cross. They concluded that Jesus died for us like the Passover lamb died for the sins of the people. Since we do not slash the throats of lambs any more next to those nice Sunday flowers on the altar, some people have a hard time with this blood and sacrifice stuff. I am one of them, but then again, it is there, so let's deal with it.

In the good old days when Scripture was being written, blood had to be spilled in order for a bold promise to be made. You could

16. Isaiah 53:5.

not just "cross your heart and hope to die"; something had to actually die to seal the deal. The word covenant in Hebrew may even derive from the word "to cut." The old sacrificial image works for many people, but the way I see it is that the love of Jesus went all the way to the valley of death to get me—and us. Jesus laid it all out there because that is what God was doing with and through him for us.

Later, all this sacrifice stuff was overlaid with other cultural understandings that came about as people struggled to understand Jesus' death. One is the *Penal Substitution* theory in which Jesus is understood as taking on the punishment that we deserved so that justice was served and God could forgive us. Another is the *Ransom* theory where God had to buy us back from the devil to whom we had been handed over because of the sin of Adam and Eve. Jesus acted as the ransom, thereby tricking the devil because you cannot keep a good man down. Another is the *Moral Exemplar* theory in which Jesus serves as the perfect example of a moral life, intended to inspire us to good works—and there are others you can look up.

There was no consensus on any of these theories. Moreover, are you getting the idea that they are a stretch, and some of them end up making Jesus' dad look quite bad? After all, does God have to be persuaded to save us by the sacrifice of his only child? Are we so far in debt that nothing can help us? Is the bankruptcy court closed? Is God so mad about how screwed up things are that someone has to die to balance the scale and that someone just has to be pretty special to get God's attention?

Mark Heim has an interesting perspective about sacrifice which is derived from the work of René Girard, an anthropologist whose thought on this subject is currently very influential in theological circles. In Heim's book, *Saved from Sacrifice*, he says:

> We are not reconciled with God and each other by a sacrifice of innocent suffering offered to God. We are reconciled with God because God at the cost of suffering rescued us from bondage to *a practice of violent sacrifice* that otherwise would keep us estranged, making

us enemies of the God who stands with our victims. We are reconciled with each other because, at the cost of suffering, God offered us an alternative to our ancient machinery of unity.[17]

Does blood mixed with violence have to be the way to salvation? Well, my answer, for what it is worth, is "no" and "yes." Jesus does willingly offer his life. He hangs from his cross for us and says to us, "This is how much I love you. When you feel hung out to dry, you are not alone. I am with you. I do this to share in and redeem your suffering. I'm not just a martyr hanging up here; I'm God's son, *the* son, and this means something to God, and we want it to mean something to you. Now I freely do this for you. What will you do with this?"

In my office there are five crucifixes. Those who come to see me think it is because my father raised me Catholic, even though I ended up being a United Methodist pastor. But that is not the reason. The reason for all those crucifixes is what I have shared with you. When broken people sit with me and ask the "why" questions and struggle to understand "the man behind the curtain," I point to one of the crucifixes, and I tell them that he hangs there for them and with them. When the questions cannot be answered by bumper-sticker, religious-sounding platitudes, Jesus hangs there for the questions. "He died for you and your questions," I tell them.

When I hold up the bread and I break it and raise the cup and say words over them, I repeat ancient words that can be heard in many ways. I offer the words in faith and trust that they will be heard in a way that will lead to faith and wholeness. But for me those words mean this: Here is the best thing God ever put together. God sent this person for the whole world, not just for the church—God so loved the *whole world*. This bread is broken because God's heart was broken one Friday afternoon for you. In this brokenness there is healing and love for you—really—now!

And this cup means that love is not love unless it is poured out. God loves us so much that God pours God's self out for us. There is no holding back. There are no conditions. God is the

17. Heim, *Saved from Sacrifice*, 320.

God of the prodigal son, and God runs to embrace you today. God wants every son and daughter home, and God will go to any lengths to get you back. This is the body of Christ broken for you, and the blood of Christ poured out for you. Come taste and see that the Lord is good, come explore, come home, and know it for the first time.

There is a scene that is a turning point in the Gospel accounts about Jesus. It is when Jesus turns to his disciples and asks, "What are people saying about me?"[18] The usual translation is, "Who do people say that I am?" After a number of suggestions, some of which make no sense, such as the resurrected John the Baptist, or the long-dead prophet Elijah, Jesus asks the really important question; "Well, that sounds all fine and dandy, but what about you?" The real-life translation of that is, "But who do *you* say that I am?"

I imagine that after some pondering and perhaps some discussion, it is Peter who jumps up and says, "I'll tell you who you are. You're the main man. You're more than that—you're Superman. You are what the whole world's been waiting for, and that's for sure." Okay, the way it sounds in the Bible is, "You are the Christ, the Son of the living God." I actually like that translation better than mine because it brings us back to the point of this chapter.

Who do *you* say that he is? If, for you, he is simply another hero in a long chain of nothing-more-than-comic-book legends, then you are probably not reading this book anyway. But if he is something more than just another hero, but you cannot swallow all the "If you don't believe in Christ and all the doctrines surrounding him in a certain way, you are going to hell without passing Go or collecting $200" stuff, then I have some good news for you.

The Jesus I have encountered in moments of searching is a different kind of Jesus. I truly believe that this Jesus is simply asking you, "Who do you say that I am?" If your answer is in the same spirit as my mentor Leslie Weatherhead, which might sound something like, "Well, I'm not so certain of all the different ways there are of understanding you, but I am compelled to find out more about you, and I somehow want to follow in the way you

18. Matthew 16:13–20.

63

offer," then come, come follow Jesus, and be willing to discover further light and bump up against some new insights and know them for the first time in a new way.

6

The Holy Spirit and Elmer's Glue

I SUPPOSE I AM dating myself by using the reference to Elmer's glue in the title of this chapter. It comes from an old song by Avery and Marsh that was put out in 1973. The implication is that there are two things you can count on finding in any church: the Holy Spirit and Elmer's glue.

The glue part is self evident; at least it used to be. Countless children, including me, used Elmer's glue to paste onto paper everything from cutouts of biblical characters to leaves and other shapes that depicted some of God's creation. The Holy Spirit part is a play on words, assuming that this mystical third person of the Trinity somehow joins together the other two parts. The Father, the Son and the Holy Spirit are forever joined as three in one by the glue of the spirit. Are you confused yet? Well, it is called the *mystery* of the Trinity, after all.

Before I get too far into describing this mystery, let me tell those of you who are reading this who might have trouble with this three-in-one image that, for three hundred years or so, many people believed in Jesus and followed him without benefit of the doctrine of the Trinity. So the good news before we delve into the mystery is that you could simply be a first- or second-century Christian and keep on keeping on.

Theologian and scientist Michael Servetus was burned at the stake long ago in 1553 when he would not believe in the Trinity because he said it was simply not biblical. So if you have a burning desire to hold on to this concept, that is fine, but let us look into it to see if it helps or hurts your concept of who God is.

Weatherhead, in his treatment of the Holy Spirit, quotes Harry Emerson Fosdick, a famous and progressive preacher of the early twentieth century, "The idea of God in three persons is difficult enough without compounding the difficulty by calling one of them a 'ghost.'"[1] Or did I forget to tell you that this third "person" of the Trinity used to go under the name of Holy Ghost? It did, and it still does in some parts. I once wrote something about the Day of Pentecost, as described in the book of Acts, entitled, "A Really Good Ghost Story."

The event happened in a room with all the doors and windows shut. The disciples of Jesus were gathered waiting for instructions from headquarters. The problem, however, was that the CEO of this newly formed company was gone. Jesus, the now-departed CEO, had told them just before he went off on an extended leave that he would send "someone" who would sort of take his place and give them their new marching orders. This "someone," he defined as the Holy Spirit.

Here begins the perception issue. What is the difference between this Holy Spirit and the now-gone Jesus? Weatherhead suggests that there is really no difference. If he is right, then why do we need the concept of the Trinity? If the presence of the resurrected Jesus is what showed up after Jesus' death and resurrection, then maybe calling this presence the Holy Ghost is in fact a better description of what showed up. I cannot help but think of Dickens' Ghost of Christmas Past as a term to describe this new phenomenon. After all Jesus did get his start at Christmas. Oh well, so much for a digression.

Now, let's get back to the really good ghost story. The disciples were waiting for something or someone to show up. The scene when the "someone" showed up looked and sounded like something whose origin was somewhere between the Bermuda Triangle and the Twilight Zone. The wind blew open the shutters, and the

---

1. Weatherhead, *The Christian Agnostic*, 146.

door swung open. Tongues of fire danced over the disciples' heads like sugarplums. Wait, wrong story.

After being lit up, they all started speaking in foreign tongues, even though Rosetta Stone had not yet been invented. The Scripture story simply states that they were "filled with the Holy Spirit."[2] This event is also known as the birthday of the church because, as a result of what happened, this same confused bunch that a month or so earlier had betrayed and deserted their CEO now went out and created all kinds of branch offices. Something sure happened. If it had not, we would not have the church today.

So what is this Holy Spirit? At first, many understood the Holy Spirit to be a different, ghostly, version of Jesus, as in the Pentecost story. It is rather like when we talk about the spirit of a departed loved one remaining in our hearts: "The spirit of Uncle John is still with us." Unlike the spirit of dear Uncle John, however, this Spirit of Jesus is much more present and powerful. Jesus promised that he would be with those who wanted to continue the business, and the Elmer's glue of Pentecost really did put back together a straggly band of followers and made of them a significant agent of change for the world.

Others understand the divine presence in a way that I might term "blender theology." This blender effect works by putting God, Jesus, and the Holy Spirit together and then pushing the "whip" button. For some people this margarita of a drink is fine. God and Jesus and whatever kind of presence one experiences when the time comes are what it is. The experience of the Holy Other is what matters, whether you call it Jesus or God or Spirit. To know that something beyond you is present with you can make a real difference, and that is what is important.

With its foundation firmly planted in the monotheism of Judaism, the early church struggled a lot to figure out how to understand the nature of Jesus and the Holy Spirit. The Emperor Constantine convened the Council of Nicaea in 325 CE to determine what was going to be the party platform about the nature of Jesus and his relation to God the Father. Dissent was threatening

2. Acts 2:4.

to split the church that centered on whether Jesus was equal in divinity to God the Father, or whether there was a time when Jesus did not exist. The majority rule of this meeting was that God the Father and Jesus were persons of identical substance. In other words, they shared the same divinity and had eternally co-existed.

It was out of this Council meeting that the Nicene Creed was formulated, but this creed did not include any details about the Holy Spirit. It was not until after subsequent Council meetings over the next hundred years or so that a further paragraph about the Holy Spirit was added to the original creed. In this revised creed, the Holy Spirit was described as "the Lord, the giver of life, who proceeds from the Father and the Son, who with the Father and Son is worshiped and glorified, who has spoken through the prophets,"[3] which are the words that are recited to this day during worship whenever the Nicene Creed is read.

Immediately after Jesus left and the Holy Spirit arrived however, I am not sure the distinctions were all that important to his first followers. They only became important later. For some modern-day people, the reasoning behind the original Trinity debate seems lost to the ages, but the result of the vote at those first conventions reverberates down through the years. Most every Sunday, when I send people out of the worship service with their marching orders, I use this Trinitarian Benediction; it is a blessing in the name of the Father, Son, and Holy Spirit.

To be honest, I like the concept of the Trinity. Maybe my liking it and the reason for liking it is a key, for those of you out there who have no use for Trinitarian language, to taking another look at this ancient doctrine. I use it in a pragmatic way. It is like the three blind men who try to describe an elephant. One man holds onto the trunk of the animal and declares it to be snake. Another holds onto the tail and says that surely it is a rope. The other man holds onto a leg and announces that what they have is a tree.

When it comes to the God of the universe, and not those little gods that we make into what we think might be God, we need to remember that we are flying blind. We do not really know what

---

3. "The Nicene Creed," *The United Methodist Hymnal*, 880.

God looks like, but we choose in faith to believe—even in the face of our not knowing and our unbelief—so what do we say?

We say what we can, but we know that what we know is formed by a limited perspective of the divine. So in the Trinitarian Benediction, God is described firstly as the one who creates. This is the traditional "God the Father" role. Okay, sure, you can use the word "Mother" if you want to upset some of those who are dead set on the parent role of God being only "Father" because Jesus and the Bible in general calls "Him" that, because as I have already mentioned, the Bible was written almost solely by men who lived in a patriarchal world view and who forgot that God is neither male nor female. But let me continue on about the benediction. The Creator is the parent part of God who can be mother or father. That is for those out there who want to hold on to the trunk.

Then there is the Son. For Christians, the Son is the real earthy Jesus who is not a once-upon-a-time kind of hero but who really did live a flesh-and-blood life. This is for the people who really like to sing, "What a Friend We Have in Jesus," and mean it. These folks have hold of the tail and relate more to a person than a big mysterious creator God who is kind of like a grandfather or grandmother in the sky. They want someone with his feet on the ground. Jesus, the Son, works well for that.

Then there is the subject of this chapter, the Spirit. This is for the mystics, for those who need to hold on to the part of God that is the beyond and the within, and they are comfortable with that. I often use the image of breath when I do this part of the benediction, and there is good precedent for that. The word "spirit" in Hebrew is *ruach*, which can mean breath, wind, or spirit.

So I often put the benediction this way, "May you be blessed in the name of the God who created you in infinite mystery in moments you do not remember . . . May you be blessed in the name of the Son, who felt all that you felt and lived and died with and for you . . . and may you be blessed in the name of the Spirit, that unseen presence and power that can allow you to do far more than you can do on your own and that is as close as your next breath." Then to wrap it up, I either say, "Now you are blessed in the name of the Father, Son, and Holy Spirit," or if I am feeling real progressive, I say, "Now you are blessed in the name of the God who created you, the God who redeemed you, and the God who can empower you."

All this is to say a rose by any other name is a rose—or was that an elephant? The Trinity is a human way of trying to picture how God is known and how God works from a Christian point of view. If this is helpful, that is good. If it is not helpful, it is not a deal breaker, in my opinion.

Of course, the above thoughts are, I believe, what is known as the heresy of modalism. To think that the Trinity is not an ontological reality but a way to define the different modes, or behaviors, of God is one of the minority reports that ended up being heresy. The picture of God in the best-selling book "The Shack," by William P. Young, does this in what I think is a wonderful fashion.

The author never claims it to be a theological work but rather a parable about God and the relationship between the three "persons" of the Trinity. God the Father is portrayed as a black woman, the Son sort of plays himself, and our topic for this chapter is portrayed as an Asian woman named Sarayu, which is a word for "spirit" in Sanskrit.

The Holy Spirit is a figure rather like the breeze and is feminine. The word for "spirit" in the Bible is often in the feminine. That should make some of you out there happy and maybe even win over a few converts who might want to take another look at this Holy Spirit thing.

In terms of heresy, I offer something that came to me on one of my morning runs. It goes along with the old show "You Might Be a Redneck if . . ." that has been popular on television. I thought about some responses to the statement that might begin: "You Might Be a Heretic if . . ." As I said earlier, I am kind of fond of some of those early church heresies. Many times the minority reports that did not make it into the party platform are worth taking a look at for what they were trying to describe.

You Might Be a Heretic if . . . :

- You believe that the Trinity is a human way of viewing the different functions of God.

- You don't think God is your co-pilot, or the man upstairs, or a cozy, heavenly grandparent who is a combination of Charlton Heston as an elderly Moses in the movie *The Ten Commandments* and Santa Claus.

- You don't think that all those who do not believe in Jesus as their "personal savior" will fry in some sort of eternal trash incinerator.

- You have a hard time believing that Jesus turns water into Merlot, or that he walks across the Sea of Galilee to have lunch at a local fish camp, or that he pulls five thousand box lunches out of a hat.

- You don't like the taste of local church Kool-Aid.

Keep reading because there is hope for you—and me. Spencer Burke and Barry Taylor, in their book *A Heretics Guide to Eternity*, recount some wisdom they heard from a rabbi:

> The Hasidic teacher Nachman of Bratislav urged his followers to give up the old, familiar things, which, he said, often comfort us but perhaps no longer transform, and to reach instead for the "thing which is beyond us," the thing we can only reach if we are willing to stretch ourselves forward, to leap into the abyss.[4].

I believe that in that leap, there awaits the presence and power of what is called the Holy Spirit; the abyss is actually full of a waiting spirit.

I personally believe that whatever and whoever the Holy Spirit is, he or she does not much care for the party platform anyway. I believe that the Holy Spirit is one of the connecting points of the otherness of God with our humanity. We have within us a receiver of sorts that can take in signals from a kind of divine

4. Burke, *A Heretic's Guide to Eternity*, 228.

transmitter. The frequency is such that the signals are not digital but, you guessed it, spiritual. It seems to me that what the Holy Spirit is for the would-be Christian is the Spirit that existed before Jesus walked on the earth, but that was imprinted by something very powerful at the resurrection. So the Holy Spirit has a lot of Jesus in it—at least for me and maybe for a lot of other people.

Breathe deeply and you encounter the Holy Spirit. In acknowledging that your abilities are not something you ordered from a catalog, you profess that they are gifts of the Spirit. The Holy Spirit is the gift-giver part of God. In God's factory, if you look in the staff directory you will find the Holy Spirit under the listing of "Creativity."

This is why the Bible tells of the Spirit brooding over creation in the very first creative act. The Holy Spirit has always been around. The Holy Spirit is bigger than Jesus, but she and Jesus sort of got "married" after Jesus got hung out to dry (so to speak). No more dating or being really good friends. At the resurrection a new creation was born much like a marriage creates a new life from what already is—and yes, it is about love.

The Holy Spirit must be pure love because the Spirit is spread all over the place. The amazing love of the Creator that was poured into the Son exploded over all creation as the Holy Spirit was set loose in the world at the resurrection. The Holy Spirit cannot be contained in a creed and cannot be captured by any one religion. The Holy Spirit is the expansive love of God.

For the Christian, the Holy Spirit contains the ongoing love of Jesus who promised that even though he had to leave the world, he would never leave us as orphans without a parent. The Holy Spirit really is as close as our next breath. It is just that most of the time we are not paying attention.

So do you need to believe in the Holy Spirit to be a Christian? Well, for sure you could be a pre-Nicene, pre-creed sort of Christian and not buy into the strange math of three in one but you might also miss a power that really seems to want to breathe life into us.

For those who lean toward the mystical way of experiencing life, the Holy Spirit is a way to experience God beyond doctrines. It is a presence that contains the warmth that is needed in the face of the mundane. Things can become cold and ordinary without a sense of the spirit that is holy. Stop now and take a deep breath. Feel life flowing through you—and when you do, you can, at the same time, smile and say hello to "Mom," and "Dad" and their "Son." It is really quite a family, and you and I are members of the family. The essence of the idea of the Trinity is relational and the "spirit" part is what keeps the family together.

We are held together not because we are alike but because of the unifying of the spirit which we all share. So it is as I said—the Holy Spirit and Elmer's glue.

7

The Church: God's Rag-tag Army

SOME OF YOU WHO are reading this may have no use for the church. Since that is where I have received my paycheck for over forty years, you may think I do not understand your stance, but I do. Some of the most wonderful as well as some of the most judgmental people I know occupy church pews. We who frequent buildings with steeples atop them, usually with a cross on top of those steeples, often do not act like the man the cross represents.

As I write this, I am tired of the constant debate about styles of worship, the authority of Scripture, or issues such as Creationism versus evolution. I am frustrated that in some cases, the church is digging in its heels when it comes to issues like gay marriage or the ordination of women. The list goes on, unfortunately. I understand why some would rather read the paper on Sunday morning while sipping a cup of coffee at Waffle House. I have actually tried that occasionally when I have a Sunday off. It feels quite good.

Of course, I am not talking about those who simply are lazy and do not want even to attempt to discover what is going on underneath those steeple-topped roofs. I am talking about those who have been wounded by the harsh words of religious-sounding people. I am referring to those who do not feel any love and acceptance coming their way from narrow-minded people who act like they/we have a monopoly on the truth. So let me at least say to you, if you are in that camp, we are not all like that.

Some think that the church was born the day that Jesus nicknamed Simon Peter "the rock." After Peter shocked his fellow disciples, and maybe even Jesus, by answering Jesus' question, "Who do you say that I am?" with the words, "You are the Christ, the Son of the living God," Jesus announced, "Upon this rock I will build my church, and the gates of Hell shall not prevail against it."[1] For some, that "rock" was Peter himself, so he was immediately given a large promotion to Pope.

For others, Jesus meant that it was Peter's statement that was the rock, so Jesus did not so quickly turn things over to Peter but kept the "keys" of the church in his own pocket for at least a while. After all, let's remember who Peter was. He was the guy who adamantly stated that the rest of those loser disciples might deny Jesus, but not "Rocky"—no, not him.

However, if you know the story, Peter is the first to chicken out on Jesus, a fact that is confirmed with a rooster crowing in the background as good old Rocky crumbles in the face of questions about his own identity. After a series of accusations about Peter being one of Jesus' disciples, Peter jumps up and shouts with angry denial, "I don't know the bum!" About that time, that fateful rooster crows, "Oh yes you do, sucker!"[2]

So with crushed rock as the foundation for an institution where the gates of Hell are no match, let's be honest that, from the get-go, the church has often found itself offering a heavenly message but getting itself in a hell of a mess. That is because the church is made up of people like Peter and me, and yet we pride ourselves in not being at Waffle House most Sunday mornings.

When I go to a new church, I always use Martin Bell's image of the rag-tag army as my introduction to my new congregation. I confess up front about who we really are. You can read the whole story in his book, *The Way of the Wolf: The Gospel in New Images.* Here is some of what I say, using Martin Bell's words:

---

1. Matthew 16:16–19.
2. Matthew 26:73–75.

> I think God must be very old and very tired. . . . He's
> been on the march a long time, you know. And look at
> his rag-tag little army! All he has for soldiers are you
> and me. Dumb little army. Listen! The drum beat isn't
> even regular. Everyone is out of step. And there! You
> see? God keeps stopping along the way to pick up one of
> God's tinier soldiers who decided to wander off and play
> with a frog, or run in a field, or whose foot got tangled in
> the underbrush. God will never get anywhere that way.
> And yet, the march goes on. . . . And even though our
> foreheads have been signed with the sign of the cross,
> we are only human. And most of us are afraid and lonely
> and would like to hold hands or cry or run away. And
> we don't know where we are going, and we can't seem to
> trust God–especially when it's dark out and we can't see
> him! And he won't go on without us. And that's why it's
> taking so long. And yet, the march goes on. . . . [3]

I consider myself a Lieutenant in this rag-tag army of sorts. It takes some of the pressure off to know I do not have to be the General. God is the one who knows where he is going and who is stopping to pick up the ones who go astray and those whose feet have gotten tangled in the underbrush.

When I was a young buck and pushing back against most everything, I used to argue with my now-deceased mother about the irrelevancy and pettiness of the church. One night she grew tired of my rebellious attitude, pointed her finger at me, and said words that I now use often, "Boy, let's get something straight. I put up with the church so that the church can be the church when the church needs to be the church."

Her words ring in my soul as she must now smile at her boy who has been "putting up with the church" for forty years or so. Her words lovingly haunt me as I reflect over the past couple of years as I officiated at the funerals of three dear members of my congregation who died well before their time. As we gathered together with hope and faith in a sanctuary full of people whose

3. Bell, *The Way of the Wolf*, 89–91.

faces were filled with pain and with so many questions, I spoke these words: "We come today to the only place we can come."

I witnessed people in the church holding on to these wounded and broken families, sharing hugs and casseroles, visiting, listening, and praying. I was able to walk with them through these darkest of times, and as a church, we were able to surround them with love in a very tangible way.

These are some of the many powerful experiences I have had of the church being the church when the church needed to be the church, and there are many more instances of the church being the church every day. Church members work on Habitat houses, serve meals to the under-resourced, support those who are going through hard times, provide financial support to many local and distant agencies that are working on behalf of the poor or marginalized, work against human trafficking, sing in nursing homes, nurture one another in spiritual and personal growth . . . The list is endless and encompasses acts of both charity and justice.

It is important to remember also the many contributions of religious leaders in history who have fought for human rights. The Bible is full of God's concern for social and economic justice; within its pages you will find the overarching message that we should do right by our neighbor. The prophets spoke in defense of the widows and the orphans, the poor and the powerless, the displaced and the marginalized.[4] The Hebrew word "mispat," which means "justice," may be found more than four hundred times in the Hebrew Bible.[5]

Jesus' mission statement was taken straight out of the book of Isaiah, who was one of the major prophets of the Hebrew Bible: "The Spirit of the Lord is upon me, because he has anointed me to bring good news to the poor. He has sent me to proclaim release to the captives and recovery of sight to the blind, to let the oppressed go free, to proclaim the year of the Lord's favor."[6]

---

4. See Isaiah 10:1–2.

5. Cannon, *Social Justice Handbook*, 19.

6. Luke 4: 18.

Those of us who follow Jesus have a mandate to follow in the footsteps of those men and women of faith who have come before us—who have fought against the injustice of slavery and economic inequality and who have been working for civil and human rights, immigration reform, environmental protection, and so on. All of this is rooted in our worship of a God who cares passionately about all of creation. Through worship, the church is renewed and refreshed to go forth and serve.

Those outside the church often do not see the church being the church as the above-mentioned community of wounded healers, nor do they necessarily have a place to come to where their vision of and for the world may be renewed and strengthened, where skewed priorities of competition, consumerism, and self-interest may be reevaluated and readjusted, and where they can be part of a community that seeks to do right to all its neighbors.

I like what Weatherhead says in his chapter on the church about those outside the church:

> There are many outside the church who ought to be in. They may feel excluded, and some exclude themselves, but Christ, I feel, would welcome them. They criticize from outside. If they would criticize *from within* with positive suggestions, their words would not be so resented and would be more likely to effect the changes they desire . . . Criticism hurled across a gulf of hostility or indifference is of far less value, and widens the gap between the church and people.[7]

Then he continues with words that I love:

> Let us try to see the Galilean standing on the beach, with the blue sky above him and the green hills behind him, the waves rippling to his feet, with the sorrows of the whole world on his spirit, but with the unquenchable joy of God in his eyes, calling to men to show the world a new way of life and reveal the beauty and glory of God. For *that* is what the church exists to offer.

7. Weatherhead, *The Christian Agnostic*, 177.

Now that is my kind of Jesus and my kind of church. Did you hear that, mom? Yes I know we can regress and be like some kind of religious club issuing guidelines for membership, but that is not what "the Galilean" had in mind. Such club-like status must have been on Weatherhead's mind when he wrote in an earlier passage:

> Actually the church can count on very few of its members really showing forth the way of Christ in the world. A high percentage of its members are not changed themselves. Therefore, of course, they have no burning message or witness for others. Many are willing to work in order to "fill the church." They have no vision of what the church exists to offer to those who fill it . . . "Come and be like us," they cry. But the man in the street says in his heart, "From ever being like you may your God deliver me!"

So, on behalf of the rag-tag army, I plead guilty, but the church still needs to be the church when the church needs to be the church. So if you are reading this book, you must have some interest in the war that this little army is waging. Give it another try. We need you. Shop around for a church that knows its rag-tag status and fesses up to it. There are a lot of churches I would not attend, but do not let that stop you from looking.

Hurting people can find shelter from the storm within the walls of the church. The rag-tag army is out there and marching to help God heal the world. So, if you have been frustrated with the church, find one that is still on the march and not sitting in the shade waiting for the Kool-Aid truck to come by.

The church I presently serve, for example, participates in many ministries in the community and further afield. From providing food and shelter during the winter for our homeless neighbors and supplying backpacks full of food for kids in local schools who would otherwise not have something to eat over the weekend, to joining in relief efforts in areas that have been struck by disaster and building up educational opportunities in Guatemala, to innumerable music, children's, family, youth and adult ministries, our church has countless opportunities to be involved in service, as well as in worship, education, and fellowship (borrowing some of the words of our church's mission statement.)

The rooster still crows, and we still so often deny what our leader so longs for us to claim, and that is why the march is taking so long, but the Galilean will not give up on us. He needs branch offices where real love and healing are offered.

We do things called sacraments to help us remember that first calling. We baptize babies as an act of radical grace. Sure, the kid does not know what is happening, but we believe God does. As parents hand me their little bundle of love, I sometimes (jokingly of course) remind them that I do not have to give the baby back to them. After their smile of surprise, I tell them that part of what they are doing is a ritual reminder that this child is a gift from God and they are bringing the baby to the baptismal font as a way of saying, "This is your child, God, on loan to us." They are bringing God's child back to God.

As the child grows up, the parents are to remind the child over and over again, "You are a child of God." Since God loves us but does not trust us, parents have to not just acknowledge this ownership, they have to take very public vows and promise God all this. When the kid gets to be a teenager and angrily says, "I don't want to go to church! It's boring," the only parental response that is necessary is, "Well, that's as may be. You have to go because I promised God that I would take you until you get old enough to say 'no' on your own. For now it's non-negotiable. I'm not messing with God."

Then there is the sacrament of Holy Communion. If you are not "in the club," what we do at Communion may sound strange or even barbaric. The early Christians were accused of being cannibalistic when word got out that they were drinking blood and eating flesh. We come to the Table of the Lord to taste and see. There are all kinds of theological ways of describing what happens when the bread and cup are blessed, but suffice it to say that they re-present Jesus in a way that is real to the participant in the sacrament.

We humans often need something more than words in order to participate in a symbol that participates in that which it symbolizes. Does that make sense? If it does not, then rack it up to mystery, because that is what happens at the Eucharist. Eucharist is another word for Holy Communion and is really a better term.

"Eucharist" comes from a word that means both *grace* and *thanksgiving.* That is about as close as one can get to describing what is transpiring at the Table. We come to say thank you to God for loving us in Jesus. We remember his death and know that we do not deserve such love—that is the grace part.

"Sacrament" comes from the Latin word *sacramentum,* which was the sacred oath of loyalty that a Roman soldier took that he would serve the emperor even if this led to his own death. So in baptism and communion we believe what seems impossible to believe; God has promised to show up when the water is poured and the bread and cup are lifted. You might say that God is around all the time, but in the sacrament, a potent, condensed version of God fills the space. God sort of says, "Don't ask for it if you don't want it. You ask and I'll show up—It is my sacred oath to do so."

Church is a place where God shows up, and if you do too, you may very well find yourself meeting God there. You may be stretched and challenged to move from where it is comfortable to places of growth and doing things you never thought possible. The church can be a place where you may find a sense of community in a world that has become progressively more individualistic and fragmented. In community, you will be able to participate in the healing and re-creation of the world more effectively than by yourself. Rag-tag the church may be, and it has a long way to go to live up to its leader's name, but the march goes on, and God will not go on without us . . .

8

The Bible: Brick or Quilt?

PERHAPS THE MOST DAMAGING words that can be hurled in the direction of a person who says, "I believe; help my unbelief!" are the words, "The Bible says . . ." The person who utters this proclamation usually then proceeds to find some kind of text that supports his or her point of view. The problem with this often-used phrase, if one really wants to understand the Bible rather than use it as a brick to be tossed at someone with whom you disagree, is that it leaves out an essential element.

The essential element is, "So what does the Bible mean when it says a certain thing?" I would offer a challenge. Think of any pronouncement about something you want to justify. If you have the time and the right tools you can find some verse or phrase in the Bible to prop up your pronouncement. This includes everything from dietary guidelines to how to parent children.

Someone recently sent me a collection of "biblical models for marriage." The phrase is often tossed around as if there is only one biblical understanding of marriage. If you do your research, you will find many types of marriage appearing in the pages of the Bible, some of which you probably would rather not know.

Indeed, the Bible says a lot of things, including the need to treat slaves with compassion and our right to stone teenagers when they sass a parent. The issue begins with what the Bible is and what it is not. Many people treat the Bible as if it were put together like a brick. A brick is created by mixing different elements together and pouring them into a mold. What comes out is a composition made up of a consistent blend of ingredients. It is about the same all the way through.

The Bible is not a brick. It is more like a family quilt pieced together by a loving grandmother. She has collected patches passed down by family members who have preceded her. Each patch represents history. Some are quite old and would never be placed in a blanket made by a machine in some factory. Such placement would seem irregular.

But this is a family quilt. Its purpose is not to look good, nor is it meant to be exactly symmetrical. It is put together with love in mind so that it can be passed down to other family members. Once it is completed, there will be rough edges because the various patches bear the markings of other hands and reflect the years of their heritage.

Noticing the individual pieces allows one to tell the family story. Not everything seems to fit because we are looking at the total pattern from our own point of view and our individual story. The quilt is meant to be wrapped around someone for warmth and even emotional support. Bricks on the other hand may be used for building but they can also be thrown at someone to make a point.

The Bible is made up of all kinds of literature, such as poetry, sermons, letters, history, and genealogy. The genre of the book should obviously be taken into consideration when it is being read. The Bible is not made of the same "stuff" throughout and definitely should not be tossed around as if it were a brick.

Another image of the Bible that I find helpful is to think of it as being like the Grand Canyon. Sometimes people tell me that they see the God of the Bible as a God of wrath who seems rather arbitrary in choosing who gets blessed and who gets cursed. You can sure find that kind of God in the pages of the Bible. Those patches were passed down by the family, so they were placed in the quilt.

But to switch the image, the layers of the Grand Canyon are what make it grand. Its ancient layers are exposed for all to see. Each layer represents what was happening at that particular point in history many years ago. If we want to fully appreciate the

Canyon as a whole, we need to explore the many different layers and all they have to teach us; we cannot just choose one layer, even the top layer, and ignore the rest.

In the same way, there are many layers of thinking about God in the Bible. Each layer represents the theological thinking of the time. When we fail to study the history of this layering, we end up not respecting the nature of the Bible. Often someone will dig into one of the layers, take some of the material, mix it in their own private mixer, pour it into a mold, and come up with a brick-like statement. The problem with this approach is that only one layer was mined, so the total meaning is missed. Such mixing and mining leads one to make a statement like, "The Bible says . . ."

If you want a historical precedent for this, you can look up a guy named Marcion, who was a Christian living in the second century. After (mis-)reading the Hebrew Bible, which, by the way, was the only Bible back then, he decided that the God that Jesus called "Abba" could not possibly be the wrath-filled God of vengeance he had seen appear in the Hebrew Scriptures.

So Marcion did a first-century version of "cut and paste." He simply eliminated the entire Hebrew Bible, despite all the other understandings of God that appear throughout, and started doing the same with the materials that would later become the New Testament. He kept only those very limited parts of Scripture that suited his view of God. Even before the day of creeds, this hack job was too much for those folks who would later wear the sweatshirts that read "Orthodox and Proud of it."

Because of his rejection of the Hebrew Bible, Marcion has also been considered by many to be anti-Semitic. In fact, some say that his ideas were appropriated by German Christians during the Nazi period.[1]

You now know one reason the books we now have in the New Testament were chosen. Someone needed to decide what was in and what was out before people like Marcion threw the baby out with the bathwater. This is literally true because Marcion in fact

---

1. Linafelt, *A Shadow of Glory*, 11.

cut out the birth narratives. They were simply too other-worldly for his Jesus.

Later on, Thomas Jefferson picked up the Marcion way of editing when he came up with what is now called *The Jefferson Bible*. His cut-and-paste version eliminated all the miracles because he thought them to be non-intellectual.

Before you criticize the likes of Marcion and Jefferson, let's all own up to our tendency to come up with our personal version of the Bible. I hear people do it all the time, especially the folks in the "Bible says" club. They will clearly point out to you instances where the Bible says whatever it is that supports their particular viewpoint, but what they leave on the cutting room floor makes for a whole other Bible.

The Bible says "Sell all you have and give to the poor," and then you can follow Jesus. Many of the "Bible says" club still have deeds to houses and titles to cars but their pocket edition of the Scriptures seems to contain only verses that support their positions in terms of social issues that allow them to discriminate against certain sectors of society.

Most cut-and-paste Bible miners are literalists. They often profess to take the Bible literally—at least the part of the Bible they carry around in their personal pocket edition. However, there is a saying going around that is usually attributed to Karl Barth, the eminent theologian, who, when asked by someone if he took the Bible literally, supposedly responded, "I take the Bible far too seriously to take it literally."

To take all parts of the Bible literally is to show disrespect for the text. It is to treat the Bible as a brick made up of the same stuff rather than to honor the text for its varied compositions and complex theological perspectives. The Bible deserves to be studied for what it is, not reduced to what some people need it to be. Such reductions are naïve and can be dangerous.

The history of the misuse of Scripture can produce volumes. In the tradition in which I am ordained, which is United Methodism, we believe that the Bible is always primary, but that it needs to be interpreted in light of reason, experience, and tradition.

To simply proclaim what the Bible says, rather than to study the Bible for what it means, is to leave out too much and reduce the Bible to too little.

Another of my favorite images of the Bible, alongside the quilt image, is one that Martin Luther came up with. His perspective was that the Bible is the cradle of the Christ child.[2] When I teach Bible studies, I often use this image. I tell the story of a very special cradle in our family. It was hand crafted by a man in the small rural church I served years ago.

My wife and I were expecting our second child, and one day Ray appeared in our driveway with the cradle in the back of his pick-up. It was a surprise gift of love that we still cherish. What makes it special is not only that it is handmade, but that it ended up containing our daughter Amanda.

If you look at this cradle today, it sits a little lopsided. Its rockers are not exactly symmetrical. If you rub your hand over the ledge that covered Amanda as she slept, you will feel some rough places along the textures of the different wood that Ray used to make it. It was not made in a factory, so it has handmade characteristics. That, and what it held, is what makes it special.

Bricks are made in factories. Family quilts and specially made cradles are rough and wonderful. Quilts surround those who hold them near with love. Cradles hold precious gifts. We need to quit throwing the Bible around like a brick. We need to cease doing our personal cut-and-paste thing with it.

Someone helped me understand the difference between using the Bible to interpret Jesus and using Jesus to help understand the Bible. To begin with the Bible means that we come up with our view of Jesus based on our concept of Scripture. We pick and choose parts that we pour into our mold, and we come up with a sort of one-dimensional Christ based on our personal theology.

To begin with Jesus and then come to Scripture usually leads to a more open view of the sacred text. The overall portrait of

---

2. The actual quotation is: "Here [in the Scriptures] you will see the swaddling clothes and the manger in which Christ is lying." From Martin Luther's *The Prefaces to the Early Editions of Martin Luther's Bible*, 21.

Jesus in the Bible is a man who welcomes most everybody and who is hard on the biblical literalists of his day who, by the way, were called Sadducees.

I love the Bible but I do not worship it. It is not meant to be a paper Pope, nor is it meant to be a brick fashioned in the shape of an idol. Its many layers and patches are to be appreciated for what they are and studied in context. Not to do so often leads to anger, hate, and narrow views of both Scripture and people.

I learned to stand up for the Bible because I have spent many years studying it. I am tired of people making the Bible into what it is not. Many of these people refuse to acknowledge the contextual nature of Scripture and long to make it into "just the simple Bible and what it says." That is not fair to Scripture and can be harmful to a lot of God's children—and we are all God's children.

The Bible can be read in different ways. I think it must always be studied in terms of its genre, who wrote it, who edited it, its original audience, its varied theological perspectives, and its use of language. There are other times when it can be picked up as you would a quilt and allowed to surround a person with the power that is within its inspiration.

One way to allow its ancient wisdom to become meaningful is to use the method called *lectio divina*. This simply means "holy reading." Read a passage one time to simply hear it. Read it a second time and notice one word or phrase that somehow reaches out to you. The third time, get real quiet and allow the mystery that is God to help you understand what that word or phrase means for your life.

Let's quit the brick throwing and spend time appreciating the patches, the layers, the love, and the different textures of the wood—Let's take the Bible seriously.

Chances are, if you are reading this, you err not on the side of taking the Bible literally, but perhaps you no longer take it seriously. Maybe too many bricks have been tossed around, and you are serious enough about your science to know that the world was not created in seven days, and that a flood could not have enveloped the whole earth, not at least while people were around to build big boats.

You probably believe as I do that our species evolved over millions of years and did not suddenly appear from a cloud of dust or a clump of clay. You know that Adam and Eve's family tree simply does not add up and that Cain had to marry somebody and was not privy to *match.com*.

But I invite you back to the negotiating table to take another look at the real Bible and not the one tossed your way by TV preachers or your friend who happens to be a fundamentalist-Bible-believing-God-said-it-and-that's-enough-for-me kind of Christian. There is another way of looking at the Bible that is characterized by an openness of heart and mind.

In his book *A New Kind of Christianity*, Brian McLaren distinguishes between two ways of understanding the Bible. Rather than expecting the Bible to be a science book, or a constitution or rulebook, he advocates looking at it as a "community library, the record of a vibrant conversation, and a stimulus to ongoing conversation."[3] He hopes that this latter approach to reading the Bible will avoid the pitfalls that conservatives tend to make in putting themselves *under* the text and that liberals tend to make by lifting themselves *over* it.

> I hope [this approach] will try to put us *in* the text—in the conversation, in the story, in the current and flow, in the predicament, in the Spirit, in the community of people who keep bumping into the living God in the midst of their experiences of loving God, betraying God, losing God, and being found again by God. In this way, by placing us *in* the text, I hope this approach can help us enter and abide *in* the presence, love, and reverence of the living God.[4]

When a Scripture is read in worship, a phrase is often used as the reader finishes the text: "This is the Word of God for the people of God." The people respond, "Thanks be to God." In other

3. McLaren, *A New Kind of Christianity*, 94.
4. Ibid., 96.

words, the reading of the text expects a response, a conversation, a dialogue. However, to proclaim that the words read are "the Word of God" does not mean that they are some kind of dictation by a divine dictator. The words are the words of a community who have tried over the centuries, often with poor results, to stay in relationship with a particular God—the God of Abraham and Sarah, David and Bathsheba, Joseph and Mary, Jesus and Mary Magdalene (that pairing has been popular of late), and you and me.

The Word of God comes from the community of God and is read so that "the people of God" for whom it is intended can be in relationship to that Word. Karen Armstrong in her book *The Bible: A Biography,* states that we must never lose the Rabbinic method of understanding Scripture. She explains that when the Temple was destroyed, the early rabbis began to see the Torah (the first five books of the Hebrew Bible) as the primary place in which to seek God's presence. They saw the text as both inexhaustible and needing constantly to be revitalized; they were always in search of new and deeper meanings. In making sense of what they read, they were guided by the principle of compassion.[5]

To think of the Scriptures as something "done," like a brick, is to disrespect the living nature of God's Word. There are many portions of Scripture that need to be challenged, wrestled with, argued over, as well as many other sections that can be simply held close like a family quilt. The Bible deserves better than it often gets.

So here again, if you have tossed out the Bible as an outdated unscientific book full of prejudicial and judgmental sayings, "come back to the place you started and know it for the first time." Come back to the real Word of God written over the centuries by the people of God. At least deal with and struggle with the real Bible not the words about it that make it into that brick.

5. Armstrong, *The Bible*, 81–84.

9

Providence and Care:
The Two Hands of God

As you read this book, perhaps your real issue is not whether or not there *is* a God but rather about what it is that that God does or does not do. Most of the people who find their way into my office and profess that they are having a hard time believing in God are, in reality, having trouble believing in a God that I do not believe in either.

Their composite view of the deity is made up much like a candy popcorn ball. Various elements from leftover childhood images are stuck together using sticky theological concepts gathered from TV, church, friends, and the usual "If God is good and powerful, why is there so much suffering in the world?" which morphs into "Why do bad things happen to good people?" Incidentally, there are many, many books on this subject. One of the most helpful is the one by the Jewish author Harold Kushner.[1]

All this sticking together creates a God who is either a real son of a gun (substitute what you were thinking, depending on how mad or disappointed you are in your composite view of God) who seems not to care, or a pretty impotent God who, for whatever reason, cannot seem to intervene when necessary. The real God is so much bigger than our images.

---

1. Kushner, *When Bad Things Happen to Good People*.

So many of these people need to reboot their inner computer when it comes to their concept of God. As I hear them describe their images of God, I am aware that the "garbage in, garbage out" analogy works for theological concepts also. They have picked up all kinds of unhelpful ideas from all kinds of places, including church, unfortunately.

One of the images I often use to help struggling pilgrims on the road of faith comes from the movie *Forrest Gump*. I have long since learned that to help people who are turned off by the institutional church one may need to use non-church images to reboot their "faith-seeking hardware."

The movie begins with Forrest walking toward a bus stop in order to wait for a ride to his long-awaited reunion with the love of his life, his Jenny. As he approaches the bench upon which he will wait and tell his life story, the camera focuses on a feather blowing about in the wind.

The feather at first lands on the shoulder of a man who is wearing a business suit and carrying a briefcase. This figure represents the world of success. Next, the feather is picked up by the breeze and lands beside the soiled running shoe of Forrest Gump. He then tells his story of grace, bad luck, unbelievable serendipitous events, heartache, business success, and other events that most hearers would not believe but which he says are quite true.

At the end of the movie, Forrest stands beside the grave of his beloved Jenny. His story has been told with all its ups and downs. Forrest is speaking to Jenny's grave. He says something like this: "Momma always said we each have a destiny, but Lieutenant Dan said we are all just floating around accidental-like in the wind. I don't know which it is, Jenny . . . but I think that maybe it's both. Maybe both are happening at the same time."

Then Forrest, who is now the father of a young boy, puts the child on a school bus. The scene resembles a time when Forrest was ridiculed in his own childhood. But this time, hope fills the screen since the young child seems confident about his day ahead. Forrest looks at his child and, in his simple, childlike language, tells his son that he will be waiting on him at this same place at the end of the day.

The music starts, which is the same music that begins the movie, and the feather again appears beside Forrest's shoe as he waits on yet another bench. The feather is picked up by the wind and it floats in the breeze. As the music becomes louder, the feather seems to grow bigger, and then suddenly it is swept into the center of the screen so that it almost fills the viewing space. Then the image is frozen for the audience. Now the feather is there for "you."

I tell this story and then I say, "God has two hands. The right hand of God is the one talked about most. It is the hand of God that is close and seems to direct our ways. But the left hand of God is the hand not often seen. It is the hidden hand of God. It is the part of God that holds the mystery and the questions."

Then I hold up a feather in my right hand and say "God has a right hand." I then let the feather float down. As it does, it moves about in the unseen "wind" of the room. I then pick up the feather in my left and say, "And God has a left hand." Then I release the feather again. As it floats in the air, I wait to let it fall where it may.

I pick up the feather and hold it out to those who are listening and I say, "We are always between the hands of God. Between those hands there is hope and mystery, and there is the wind, which in Hebrew is *ruach*—wind, breath, and spirit." I then play the theme music from Forrest Gump and allow people to ponder the providence and mystery of being held in the hands of God. The feather is always coming our way.

We live in the midst of a good deal of mystery when it comes to just what God does and does not do. The God of a good deal of the religion I encounter is a God where there have to be answers; not to have some kind of answer implies that God is not in control. But what if God's control is the kind that comes with love rather than with coercion? God loves us enough to grant us freedom, and once that is done, God is not in control as much as some would need God to be. Weatherhead spends a lot of time with this idea in one of his other books, *The Will of God*.

For some people God is not God unless God can do most anything God wants. A God who cannot do it all is not God. But what of a God who chooses the way of freedom and love rather than power and force? What of a God of the limits that come with love?

So is this God helpless to do anything? I believe that God is always for us, but because of love and freedom, some things happen that God does not desire to happen. The reason that there has to be something beyond this life is that ultimate justice often does not come to fruition on this side of what we call eternity. God is not finished, and this life, as wonderful as it can be, is not all there is—more about that later.

God is always on the side of the good. It is God's nature. When the mystery of bad things envelops us, or the ones we love, we can blame God, be angry with God, or even curse God. The God we curse is the God we make up, the God we need to be in total control. It is a God who will not be what we sometimes need God to be. As Job learns, we have to stand before the mystery and either affirm a God who is often beyond our understanding, or we can say, "Forget it; I'll take my chances."

Personally I will take my chances on a God of two hands who will never let go of us, but who does not hold us so tightly that we will not get hurt. The wind still blows and that wind is full of breath and spirit and mystery—but that wind is also full of the real God.

Sometimes, like that feather, we feel like "grasshoppers blown on a windy coast." At other times our feather lands on a safe place where we can know that it is that very wind that not only gave us life but that holds us up when we are falling.

God has two hands . . .

So the above phrase was the last one I wrote before I went to bed. They were the ending to the chapter as of last night. Then words came to me in the middle of the night: "That's not enough."

Okay . . . is that you, God? . . . or a dream? . . . or my imagination? . . . or my literary conscience informing me that a chapter on "what can God do and not do" needs more words than what I had come up with? Well, the answer is "Yes."

The truth is that I have been using words to talk about God for over forty years; it is my profession after all. I know the limits and the power of using words about God. There are never enough words, and often I feel I cannot find the right words. But you have to try. It is important after all.

At 4:00 this morning, my wife asked why I was up. I simply said, "Well, I'm writing about God, and it's important, and it's not enough. I mean this is God and I have to be careful." She looked at me and did not respond.

The thing that came to me in the middle of the night has to do with our effort to communicate with God. Our attempt to gain access to the mystery we call God may be the ultimate issue when it comes to what the real God can and cannot do. Is it true that because of freedom and love, as I stated earlier, there are things that God simply cannot do, no matter how much we ask?

I believe God wants to do many things. I believe God does not desire that we continue to kill each other with handguns, or drones, or AK-47s, or suicide bombing vests worn underneath the clothes of children. I believe God grows tired of seeing children starve who could have enough food and seeing mothers die because the water that they drink and that they give to their babies is full of disease.

I believe God aches as I stand beside the grave of an eight-year-old. I believe God detests the sound of the word "cancer." I believe God feels it when a man strikes the face of the woman who years earlier he promised "to love and to cherish."

So what is the deal? The deal is that God is involved. God wants goodness for all God's children. So when we ask God to change things, I believe God does pay attention, because God cares. Yes, the God of the universe whose mysterious power created the Big Bang really cares.

When the doctor told my wife and me that the reason our seven-year-old daughter was having stomach pain was that the x-ray showed a mass in her abdominal cavity, you bet I prayed. I had heard the word "mass" too often and I knew it often meant the beginning of the end.

As I said, or rather groaned, my prayers, my head kicked in and spoke to my heart. "What do you really think you are doing? Don't you believe that God loves Abigail already? Are you begging God that the one who fashioned the universe millions of years ago will somehow stop for a moment in the midst of ongoing creation and reach down and magically make that mass go away?"

"Or are you praying for courage for yourself to face whatever is coming? Are you praying that the doctor made a mistake? Are you praying for help in what you are going to say if the next doctor's visit makes for even more bad news? After all, it's Easter in a few Sundays. What are you going to preach about on Easter if you are facing a mass that is vaster than any empty tomb?"

Of course I prayed all of this because prayer is simply being who you are with who God is. Prayer is leaning into the mystery of the universe and believing that the mystery is full of caring personality. Freud would love such language because it would prove his theory that God is really just a projection of our needs, especially when we are scared and dependent.

But, to hell with Freud. I needed to pray to something, and that something to whom I prayed, I believe with all my heart and most of my skeptical mind, *is* personal. So what happened?

The only answer I received to my groans and prayers was a sort of simple phrase that came to me while I sat still: "It's okay."

I fought back as I usually do. "What do you mean, it's okay? . . . Do you mean she's okay? . . . Do you mean that, no matter what happens, I will be okay? . . . that we will be okay? . . . that I'll still be able to put words together on Easter Sunday if my little girl is facing death? . . . What the heck does 'okay' mean?"

The next visit, the doctor, whose name I do not remember because he sure missed out on the course in bedside manners, simply said, "Well, I don't know how to tell you this but we just read the last set of x-rays and the mass is not there anymore . . . not sure what it was . . . could have been a kink in a bowel or something. You folks have a good day." Then he walked out.

So a week later on Easter Sunday, I sure had preaching material. But I knew I had to be careful, just like I woke up in the middle of the night with knowing I needed to be careful with the words of this chapter.

I told the "okay" story. Then I looked at my people and I said, "Okay means that no matter what happens, the God of Easter was there. If the news had been bad and we had lost Abigail, then the Jesus who stepped into all the unfairness and died our death would hold on to Abigail and, if need be, would have completed her incomplete life.

"I would have somehow been okay because God feels our helplessness and pain and will simply not leave us to grieve alone . . . I would have found words to say to you today if the news had been bad because I've been with countless people where the mass did not go away. Easter is about a God who says from the depths of the darkness of death, 'I am the real God—not Santa Claus or a cosmic magician. I am the wounded, personal God of the cross with all its suffering and unfairness and I will not be defeated by death. Death is mine and I will do something with it. It's okay.'"

So here is what my middle of the night words mean. Our attempts to communicate with, or even influence, God mean that we lean into the mysterious presence that is God. Our leaning can be in the form of deep breathing to get into touch with the God in us or it can be the begging of a desperate parent. We participate with the spiritual dimension of life when we pray. Something happens that will not happen if we do not pray.

No, masses do not always go away, but when we pray, we align our lives that are often out of alignment with the eternal spirit that breathes life into us. We join God in the healing and balance of this universe when we pray. It really makes a difference, no matter if we get what we pray for or not. God always pays attention. God is always for us. When we pray, God can help us more than if we do not pray because of our willingness to share our spirit with God's spirit.

Life at its base is spiritual. Some scientists, such as Nobel laureate George Wald, now believe that the pattern that is revealed at the sub-atomic level of the universe is more like mind than like a scientific/mathematical formula of sorts.[2]

Did you hear that? Creation has mind behind it and within in it, so when we pray, our mind, which is far deeper than our brain, participates with the mind that created everything—and that created you. It is okay.

So now that I am awake, is this enough? Is it enough to know that what God does is participate with us? Is it enough to know that God is not so much the man behind the curtain pulling levers and spinning wheels to create an illusion of power but a very personal creator who is with us in the joys and battles of life?

This God is both working for good and constantly trying to align the universe for balance and wholeness. And yes, it appears that this God needs and expects help from us. For some this language goes too far. To speak of a God who needs help may sound like heresy, but remember who is writing this.

If you have ever been a parent and know the deep feeling of hoping that your child will actually participate in the ongoing search for balance and wholeness that you long for them to attain, then you know what I mean. Often parents have more power than their children, but there comes a time, if real growth and maturity are to happen, that the parent has to offer guidance and then hope that the child "gets it" enough to participate in the needed growth.

Parents are not magicians or machines, neither is God. So keep on keeping on when it comes to communicating with God. It affects God and it makes a difference in you.

(I will offer more in a later chapter on prayer.)

---

2. Wald, "Life and Mind in the Universe" *The International Journal of Quantum Chemistry*, 1–15.

10

Heaven and Hell: Either-Or/Both-And/None of the Above

BY NOW, SINCE YOU are still reading this, you will not be surprised if I tell you I do not want to believe in hell. A person recently left the church I now serve "because," she informed me, "we need to hear more about hell." Well, you are not going to hear it from me. So it was a surprise years ago when, at a conference, I told the theologian Gusto Gonzalez privately of my struggle to believe in hell. He dismissed my concern almost casually by saying, "Oh yes, there has to be a hell because some people will not be comfortable in the Kingdom."

I was looking for theological underpinnings for my liberal, progressive thinking, and here one of the "good guys" was telling me there was going to be hell. Of course, I now know what he was getting at: Because of the love and freedom I have been hammering on in all these chapters, there has to be the same freedom in eternity to not choose God and the way of love.

My friend Bill used to tell me in late-night conversations that, though he claimed to be a Christian, he believed in reincarnation because he felt that no human could learn all that needed to be learned one time around. According to him, we have to come back until we learn what it means to really be human.

A note that Bill's daughter found in his files after his death indicated that he wanted me to do his funeral. Bill had written that he wanted "a hell of a party" at his daughter's home. He wanted me to read some passages from "his teacher's book" and some Scripture of my choice, and then he wanted to have his ashes scattered over the same rose bush in the back yard where his dear wife's ashes had been scattered.

So I did as instructed. I read from the book he always used to quote from, I picked some Scriptures that I thought Bill might like, and then I held up the urn that contained his ashes. I told those gathered at Bill's daughter's house about the late-night discussions that Bill and I used to have about heaven and reincarnation, about whether there would be any kind of judgment time or purgatory interval, and about the concept of hell. We wondered if we would just keep coming back until we got it right.

Just before I poured Bill's ashes over the rose bush, I looked up to the sky and said, "Well, Bill, only you now know who was right about all this, so wherever you are, or whoever you are, have a good trip." Then we had that hell of a party and told "Bill stories."

So what is it with the heaven and hell and judgment thing? Both-and/either-or/none of the above? I mean, the "either-or" thing comes into play because most everyone likes the idea of heaven if they get to go. But, then again, most of us do not like the concept of hell, unless maybe you go to one of those churches that put on Halloween hell houses. These are a type of haunted house—set up as an evangelization technique—that people walk through and watch graphic scenes of people being tortured in hell for participating in various kinds of "sin."

No wonder large groups of people stay away from church. Such graphic portrayals of the consequences of not being "their kind of Christian" are really a bad advertisement for what Jesus started with his small group of followers. They are an example of how the concept of hell has been used through the years to scare people into belief. The hell houses are biblical malpractice at its best, or worst—depending on your perspective.

Some people may believe that heaven is simply wishful thinking by people who are afraid of death. And there are those in our multiple choice offerings who simply say "live and let live," and check "none of the above."

Rob Bell's book, *Love Wins: A Book about Heaven, Hell, and the Fate of Every Person Who Lived* is, as of this writing, the latest in hell-denying literature that has many evangelical Christians rallying around the "Don't you believe it for a moment" banner. For some, to take out the concept of hell as a place of punishment in the afterlife negates the trump card of the Christian faith. After all, why be good if the "turn or burn" stuff is not real? For Bell, however, hell is the evil and woundedness, both personal and societal, that is present in our current existence.[1]

So let me simply say, in order to save a lot of words, "What kind of God needs a hell?" It is a scorekeeper God, the God of a religion that must make sure that some are down so others can be up, a God of security based on the idea that some must get their just deserts in the end. This is not the kind of God that Jesus revealed to us.

At the same time, it is true that the Bible is one hell of a book or, to put it in nicer language, the Bible does contain references to something we have translated as hell. So let's give the devil his due—oh yes, we are going to have to deal with that rascal too if we want to be honest about hell. But there again, we need to examine references to the devil in Scripture in context. The current pitchfork-carrying inflictor of nasty stuff should be reserved for cartoons because you will not find that guy in the Bible. The idea of a devil as a powerful counter-deity is simply not found in the oldest Scriptures.

One of the early references is to "*The* Satan," the character that appears in the Job story in the Hebrew Bible. *The Satan,* whose name means *the accuser,* or *the adversary,* is simply a member of the heavenly council who takes an adversarial stance with God and strikes a bargain to tempt poor old Job to curse God.[2] In this story, God is clearly convinced there is no way that one of his first-round draft picks will lose him the game. The Satan replies that

1. Bell, *Love Wins,* 63–93.
2. Job 1:7.

God is quite wrong and that if enough bad things happen to this very good person, Job will give us a preview of what Simon Peter would later do around an evening fire years later when he shouted, "I never knew the guy."

God looks at the Satan and says some words that you and I had better hope are part of a dramatic moment on stage: "You're on, Satan. Have at it with my boy Job. Do whatever you want with him, but leave him alive so that I can prove you wrong." Likely, this was a stage play whose purpose was to counter the popular theology of the day that said, "If you are good and love God, all will be well, and if bad things happen in your life, you messed up."

In fact, scholars say that the Book of Job was written to challenge that thinking about God and that it reflects the efforts of the Jewish people to understand the nature of God's providence after a time of extreme suffering. Such writing is called "wisdom literature" because we sure need this kind of wisdom when it comes to what God does and does not do—but it *is* but a story. If God is like the God we see in the first chapter of Job, I want to work for another deity.

God is not an arbitrary ruler, picking people whom the devil can tempt just to prove a point. If God is like that, we are all in trouble, and the plot of the movie *The Exorcist* is factual. In this movie, the devil picks an innocent little girl to be the one possessed. Her number comes up. She does nothing to deserve being taken over by evil; nonetheless, she is embroiled in a series of horrific acts, her head spins around, and she growls like a mad dog.

The devil does not have the kind of power we read about in the Book of Job or see in the movie. The movie is a movie, not a documentary, and the book of Job is a piece of literature that uses a set of characters to portray the challenge of a man who lost most everything and struggled to remain faithful. In the struggle he asked questions that others who wrestle with the purpose of life would ask in the future. The Satan in this old divine drama is one of the actors on the set with God. His power was inflated for the purpose of the play, but he is not real in the same sense that God is real.

To the ancient Hebrew mind, God was responsible for everything, both good and bad. It was only later—when monotheistic Hebrew thought bumped up against Persian dualism—that there arose the need for some other power to represent the dark side. When this need arose, it was set alongside a history of religions that already had a resident demon or demons, and suddenly a whole host of images of the devil appeared. So the idea of the devil is an evolutionary concept that developed in stages in the Bible. The same is true of the concept of hell, of which there is no mention in the older parts of the Bible.

The idea of hell had a foreshadowing in a place called *Sheol*, which is referred to in various places in the Hebrew Bible. Sheol is a little bit of heaven-lite plus hell with no fire.[3] It was considered the murky place where dead people went and hung out but did little. Sheol was a kind of eternal basement where no one would really like to go. For years, Sheol was mentioned in the Bible but not really talked about. Later in the continuing evolution of thinking about eternal life, heaven was elevated and hell became furnished.

Around the same time that heaven became something more than just some realm above the clouds, the biblical word for the concept that we translate as hell became *Gehenna*. Gehenna got its name from the Valley of Hinnom outside Jerusalem, where one could find flesh burning from leftover animal sacrifices and various hungry dogs "gnashing their teeth" as they turned one man's garbage into one animal's lunch. This was also the valley where human sacrifice had been conducted years before Jerusalem became the religious center for the Hebrew people, and so it was considered to be a cursed place.

You can see then that the image of a place of burning flesh and gnashing teeth was readily available to those who wanted to get the listener's attention. Jesus himself used this image, but that does not mean that this fiery place has an eternal reality. Jesus used many images in an exaggerated way including cutting hands off, plucking eyes out, and camels going through needles.

---

3. Job 21:13 says, for example, "They spend their days in prosperity, and in peace they go down to Sheol."

In addition, many people in Jesus' day did believe in a literal place called hell. Since Jesus spoke about this place, some interpreters assume he also believed in it. My opinion, however, is that although Jesus did use the language of his day, the total picture of the man who stood up to, and against, much of the religious teaching of his day would indicate that not all our chances are used up when we face judgment and accountability.

Jesus spoke of the lake of fire where the devil and his angels reside, but the man of unconditional love who told stories like the one about the prodigal son simply does not seem to me the kind of man who would condemn people to spend eternity with the devil and his angels.

Hades is another word for hell. It is the Greek version of the place somewhere down in the earth where destructive things happen. Both Hades and Gehenna got blended together into what we now think of as hell. As time went by, hell took on the threatening status that it "enjoys" today. It seems the church discovered that such a threatening place is good for business. If you want to know more about this evolution of hell, you can read *The History of Hell* by Alice K. Turner.

The concepts of heaven and hell got a lot of help during what is known as the Intertestamental period, a span of about 400 years between the writing of the Hebrew Bible and the New Testament. During that time many of the apocryphal books were written. Protestant Bibles do not typically include these books. One of these books is the Book of Enoch, which is also considered apocalyptic writing. During the early years of Christianity, a lot of Jewish apocalyptic writings were embraced by the early Christians. Apocalyptic writings, by the way, are those that often deal with visions, particularly of end times. The book of Enoch is one place you can look to find the devil, because you really will not find him in most of the Hebrew Scriptures.

Leftover apocalyptic images got picked up in the New Testament and they are scattered throughout the books of the New Testament like salt and pepper—you know, for flavor. But such images are not the main ingredients of the teaching of Jesus. Jesus was more interested in the "here and now" than the afterlife and in offering a new way of living that brought closer to reality the Kingdom of God he kept talking about.

Jesus told his disciples who sometimes had heaven on their minds that he would take care of that and that their job was to make life better now. The way he made this clear was to announce that the Kingdom was "at hand," or "in their midst." His prayer for "the kingdom to come" and "God's will to be done" was not a hoped-for dream for the future but an imperative to participate in now.

Jesus announced that his coming was a sign that it was time to sign up to be kingdom building now. The bricks and mortar of the kingdom were acts of justice and mercy, shown especially to those who were on the margins of life: the naked, the hungry, the poor, the outcasts.

Jesus offered "membership" in this kingdom to all who would see that the face of God was on those who longed for hope and justice. "Do it to the least, and you do it to me," he once said. The kingdom was also the "kin-dom." When you feed the hungry, clothe the naked, and offer a cup of cold water in Jesus' name, you become part of the kingdom family. All people are now your "kinfolk."

I like what Richard Rohr writes about all this:

> This change of frame and venue is called living in the "kingdom of God" by Jesus, and is indeed a major about-face. This necessitates, of course, that we let go of our own smaller kingdoms, which we normally do not care to do. Life is all about practicing for heaven. We practice by choosing union freely—ahead of time—and now. Heaven is the state of union both here and later. As now, so will it be then. No one is in heaven unless he or she wants to be, and all are in heaven as soon as they live in union. . . . [But] If you accept a punitive notion of God, who punishes or even eternally tortures those who do not love him, then you have an absurd universe where people on this earth end up being more loving than God! God excludes no one from union, but must allow us to exclude ourselves in order to maintain our freedom. Our

word for that exclusion is Hell, and it must be maintained
as a logical possibility. There must be a logical possibility
of excluding oneself from union and to choose separation or superiority over community and love. No one is
in Hell unless that individual himself or herself chooses
a final aloneness and separation.[4]

In other words, maybe there does have to be some kind of hell
since humans have the freedom to reject God's love and grace. But
I agree with folks like Rob Bell and Richard Rohr that God never
gives up. So even though United Methodist ministers don't typically talk about purgatory, I do like the idea.

Fire in the Bible is often meant to be a refining fire rather than
consuming fire. It could be that we all have some more learning
and refining to do before we enter whatever heaven is. Purgatory
might be continuing education on an eternal level. The fire of purgatory would be a refining fire not a consuming fire. Nothing is
gained by burning up the learner.

I wrote this a few weeks after the unbelievable massacre of
children in Newtown, Connecticut. As I was writing and thinking about this tragedy, I was imagining you might be saying
something like, "Are you telling me that the guy who shot all
those young children is not going to get punished? And are you
suggesting that those innocent little children are not going to be
somehow given justice?"

What I am suggesting is that the real God is not stupid, and
that balance and justice are hopefully part of the fabric of the universe; however, the very mentally ill young man who sprayed bul-
lets all over those classrooms is also a child of God. God will have
to do something with him. Throwing him in a burning garbage
can does not do anybody any good. God will have to help him heal
and learn. He and his arsenal cannot enter the Kingdom.

So with this very lost young man, I conjure up an image I
once used when someone challenged me about hell and Hitler. "If
you don't believe in hell, what about Hitler?" the person shouted.
"I'll tell you where I think you'll find Hitler," I responded. "He is

4. Rohr, *Falling Upward*, 101–102.

just outside heaven listening to the stories of each one of those he murdered, one at a time. If you read your history, this will take a while. If you want to call that hell, then do so, but I call it the beginning of redemption and healing for both Hitler and for the many people he destroyed."

I may be really wrong, but the misguided young man who murdered those school children must learn their stories. If heaven is about healing and "no more tears," then there is a lot of healing to do and a lot of tears to dry.

As for the children, God is brokenhearted and will need to complete their lives, otherwise God is not just nor is creation balanced. Suffering and evil win if God does not do something on the other side of life. A basic Christian teaching is that there will be accountability and there will be ultimate healing. What we have in the Bible are images of that accountability and healing, but they are only images and should not be taken literally.

But we want control and we want certainty, especially when it comes to things like heaven and hell. Our need for control bumps up against mystery. We do "see through a glass, darkly" as it says in the Bible[5] and all of our huffing and puffing cannot tear down the house of mystery that is part of real faith.

For what it is worth, I have always thought of eternal life as a space-time dimension, which is as close as the space between our thumb and our next finger if we hold them as close as we can without touching. In Celtic spirituality there are "thin places" where, if we pay attention, we can peer into the depth of reality that is beyond. This is what I think happens in those life-after-life experiences when people die and come back to tell about not only what they saw as they died, but also give glimpses of light and heaven.

These people simply step through a thin place, but they come back. As a pastor for over forty years, I have been with dying people and have experienced many thin places. All I can tell you is that something is there and it is very close.

So let me offer two last images about heaven and hell. Martin Bell writes about the parable of the wheat and the tares that is

5. 1 Corinthians 13:12.

found in the Gospel according to Matthew.[6] The wheat and the tares, or weeds, are allowed to grow up alongside each other until the time of harvest, when the wheat is gathered and the weeds burned. Martin Bell says that if this story is an illustration of how, at the end, God will burn up the hurt, the pain, and all the bad things in our lives, then it is a good story, but if the story is about God burning up people, it is a terrible and untrue story.[7] I agree with him on this.

When it comes to heaven, my favorite image is when Jesus says to a bunch of scared-to-death disciples something like, "Do not be so troubled. I'm gonna go prepare a place for you, and you'll be fine. In my Dad's house there are many dwelling places."[8] So if you want a good image of heaven, think of what a real dwelling place is for you.

For me it is the remembrance of my grandmother's front porch. Grandma Hattie had a screened-in front porch near Biloxi, Mississippi. In the days before air-conditioning, she placed a Sear's oscillating fan on one end of the porch. There were twelve rocking chairs facing each other where people could rock and drink coffee from the two large pots that were always on in her kitchen.

Drinking hot coffee and sweating while rocking in front of that continually blowing fan were as close to air-conditioning as you could get back then. You might find most anybody on that front porch because everyone was welcomed no matter who you were. One day I remember that in one rocking chair sat the town drunk, and at the other end of the row of rocking chairs rocked the Governor of the State of Mississippi. Each was drinking coffee. Each was rocking. Each was talking to my grandmother. And each was loved and accepted.

What made it a dwelling place was the welcome that was always extended, the cup of coffee that was freely given, and the amazing and accepting love of Grandma Hattie. That is heaven to

6. Matthew 13:24–30.
7. Bell, "The Way of the Wolf," 93.
8. John 14:1–2.

me. Do you have a favorite dwelling place like that? Imagine it and that is about as close to heaven as you are going to get—for now.

As for an image of hell—well—lock the door on the porch, shut off the fan, empty the coffee, and have someone standing on the front steps with a message that says something like, "You are not quite ready for such hospitality. Come with me down the street to a waiting room where God will be preparing some lessons for you. After your learning you will be able to both enjoy and appreciate what you'll find on God's front porch."

"God's Front Porch" is the title of a sermon I preached years ago about the prodigal son story. The image comes from what I imagine the father in the story doing every evening. He stands there alone looking down the road waiting for his lost child to come walking down that road.

Most evenings he goes to bed with tears in his eyes because he cannot reach his lost child until the boy has learned for himself the hard and awful lesson that his pain must teach him. But then, one afternoon as the sun is setting, the father sees a silhouette of a lone figure in the distance. At first he thinks it is his imagination—all mixed up with longing—that is playing tricks on his old eyes.

Then the figure comes close enough for the old man's eyes to focus. It is his lost child. According to the norms of the culture into which Jesus told this story, that child was dead. A request for an early inheritance meant that the son considered his father dead as well. For the father to even think of taking him back after what he had done was a mockery to all that was sacred in the family system.

I can imagine the thoughts that might race through a father's mind in this situation: What will happen if this gets out? How many other sons will ask for their inheritance before it is time and in so doing undermine the authority base of the family structure? If I take the boy back, will all my neighbors reject me?

This father does not care about the expectations and norms of the prevailing culture. The old man breaks into a run toward the figure that now is standing frozen on the road. In that culture, old men were not to run because it exposed their legs—which was a shameful thing to do according to the rules of the day.

Shame is left in the dust as the old man runs toward his boy. He embraces his lost child, and you can bet the scene is the first item on the evening news. Those watching shake their heads and think, "What is our world coming to? Nothing is sacred anymore. Family values are in the toilet."

The old man throws a party that no one in the area will attend. The father cannot even get his eldest son to come to the party because that son has joined everybody else in thinking that the old man has both lost his mind and flushed any sense of dignity and order down the drain.

To me, this story is a window through which to look at the concepts of heaven and hell. The lost child still reaps what he sows. He cannot gain back the inheritance he lost in the far country. The father allows the child to leave because love always contains freedom. The father hurts for the child but cannot learn lessons for him. In this way, accountability is still present when the father wants to put a ring on his finger and kill the fatted calf.

Nonetheless, the giving of the ring indicates that the lost boy is still part of the family, no matter what. The killing of the fatted calf and the throwing of a party reveals the real nature of the father. He is not keeping score. He has no book in a drawer somewhere to look at in the end in order to get even. He loves the child despite the child's misuse of freedom.

What the father cares about is having his child back home. Perhaps on late nights as the story continues beyond Jesus' telling of it, the now-found boy can have some conversations about the lessons he learned in the far country. As the son looks down at the scars now etched on his arms from working in the pig pen, he can talk over what those scars have taught him with a father to whom he is now willing to listen. The front porch on which they rock and talk is a dwelling place. It always was, but the child did not realize it so he strayed.

There is justice in this story, but not the justice of the people surrounding the father. They want revenge and payment for sins committed. They would want Jesus to go into a hellfire-and-damnation sermon that would end with the lost child being tossed into the lake of fire. That would be a lesson for him and for all who would hear and fear the wrath of the father.

But Jesus does not offer that kind of justice. The father of Jesus is a God whose love is revealed in a desire to have all his children home—now and later. That is the Jesus I offer to those who read this who think they cannot drink the Kool-Aid.

Jesus tells the story not just about any father. Jesus tells the story about *his* father. Jesus clearly means for the father in the story to be God. This God is the God of all people, and the God of the seeker, and of the Christian skeptic, the one who knows he or she cannot know all there is to know but who longs to believe in this kind of God and this kind of Jesus.

This kind of God wants justice in the universe and knows that we reap what we sow and that we must eventually learn our lessons. But this kind of God also wants all God's children to find home—to find at last a dwelling place.

I rest my case . . .

11

Salvation: Did Jesus Really Say "My Way or the Highway"?

"WHEN I WAS A child . . ."—it is with these words that I begin this sentence and this chapter. When I was a child . . . I was introduced to this thing called the Christian faith, and even then it did not make sense to me that all who believed in Jesus would be "saved" and all those who did not would be "forever lost."

In the limited understanding of my childhood, the math did not make sense. Could it be that simply because people do not believe in a certain figure, no matter how important that figure, their total lives, no matter how lived, would be deleted? Questions popped up in my little mind such as, "What kind of God would do this?" and "What kind of man, however important he was, would be content to know he was the cause of so many being lost?"

In my childhood, to ask such questions was not allowed. The closest answer that was given was something like, "Now you see why it is so important to spread the gospel so that everyone will have the chance to decide for Christ." Such an assertion did not help my childlike concern.

Then I began to have further questions, such as "What about those who do hear the gospel but who say "no" because they already have a different religion?" You can see from my thoughts that I was getting older and starting to think more. The answers to these questions were even more unacceptable. They basically came in one phrase, "Tough luck for them."

So let me stop this progression and explain the first phrase of this chapter. As I started writing it, the phrase reminded me of that rather famous line in one of Paul's writings, "When I was a child, I spoke like a child, I thought like a child, I reasoned like a child; when I grew up I put an end to childish ways."[1] Well, the faith given to me as a child seemed to be childish. Where was the growing up part? What kind of God writes off all those who do not believe in Jesus? To me it is a God of childish ways who says something like, "If you do not play my game, I'm going home."

So let me get a little personal here, as if I have not been that way throughout this book. I am a Christian pastor; I am not a rabbi, or a Muslim cleric, or a Buddhist monk. I believe Jesus is the incarnation of God. I believe the man Jesus is as much of God as God could put in a human being. I believe Jesus came to show us a way of life that, yes, is, "the way, the truth, and the life."

I have given my life and my career to that man and to that cause. But I cannot believe nor offer a Jesus who says, "My way or the highway." I told God this when I felt God calling me into the ministry. I said clearly to God, "If you need a preacher who is going to say on your behalf, 'Believe in my son or you will be lost forever,' then get somebody else. I do not believe that nor can I preach it."

I then waited for an answer. Having heard none, I took silence as permission to preach a gospel that offers Jesus' way of life without proclaiming that everyone who does not claim Jesus as their personal savior is lost. I believe it is God's business to love and care for all those who do not claim Jesus. I will tell the story to everyone who will listen. I have been doing it for forty-one years. A lot of people have listened and I celebrate that. They have not listened to a message of exclusivism that celebrates that half of the world is lost.

So, as directed by Scripture, when I grew up, I put away childish things and thought about some of the doctrines of the Faith

1. 1 Corinthians 13:11.

that seem to create obstacles to the journey that one needs to take in order to be a pilgrim on the road. One of those obstacles is a passage that is often used to support the opposite of what I have suggested thus far.

It comes from the lips of Jesus, or at least it comes from the Gospel writer John's version of what Jesus says. To study Scripture as I have studied it in order to be a United Methodist pastor is to try to come to grips with what the Gospels are and what they are not. As I have stated in the chapter on the Bible, it is important to not only deal with what the Bible says but to wrestle with what the Bible means.

Jesus plainly says in the Gospel according to John, "I am the way, and the truth, and the life; no one comes to the Father except through me."[2] For many people that is the banner under which they stand to state that Jesus is the only way to salvation and therefore the only way to heaven. However, to study this text is to discover that it does not mean exactly that.

First of all, as with the other three Gospels, we must realize that we are dealing with the specific theological viewpoint of the writer. Additionally, the Gospel of John, written towards the end of the first century, is full of symbolism and metaphor and is characterized by the interweaving of story with theological interpretation.

For John, Jesus is the God-Man straight from heaven, the Logos, the Word made flesh, or in the words discussed in chapter 5 of this book, the "Cosmic Christ," the "Christus," the very power of God present in creation. John 1:3 says, "All things came into being through him, and without him not one thing came into being. What has come into being in him was life, and the life was the light of all people."

Almost everyone in John's Gospel is described as being "in the dark." John proclaims that Jesus came bringing light into the world. Without the revelation of God that we have in Jesus, we would not have the particular understanding of God that we do. The Pharisee Nicodemus comes to Jesus in the dark trying to

2. John 14:6.

figure out exactly who Jesus is. After some words about the necessity of being reborn, or born from above, and about God's love for the world, Jesus concludes his interview with Nicodemus by telling him that whoever lives by the truth comes into the light; in other words, those who are living according to the way of Jesus are living in the light.

Jesus is the light of God who illuminates who God is. Jesus' character, his life, and his death are a vivid illustration, literally an embodiment, of God to the world. So when Jesus says that the only way to the Father is through him, he is saying that through him is revealed a unique manifestation of the nature of God.

Marcus Borg, in his book *The Heart of Christianity: Rediscovering a Life of Faith*, says that "the way" that John speaks of is "what we see incarnate in Jesus: the path of death and resurrection." For Borg, the way of Jesus is "dying to an old way of being and being raised to a new way of being, one centered in God," and as Borg points out, "this is the way that is spoken of by all the major religions of the world."[3]

Jesus does not say that all other ways to God are dead-end alleys. Perhaps John would say that those who do not follow the way of Jesus are already "condemned" because they are in the dark. But are they condemned to eternal damnation? The answer is no. They are in the dark because they do not live in the light, and are not following the way of love and compassion that characterizes a life centered in God—and this could apply to anyone of any religion.

Do we really think that God is limited to the Christian understanding of God? And that the Christian understanding is limited to the understanding that comes in one verse of Scripture from a particular theological understanding presented in one Gospel? In this same theological understanding, John's Jesus clearly states that "God did not send the Son to come to condemn the world but in order that the world might be saved though him."[4]

First of all, it seems that God is interested in saving the whole created order, not just the church, or just the Christians. "God so

---

3. Borg, *The Heart of Christianity*, 111.

4. John 3:17.

loved *the world* that he gave his only Son, so that everyone who believes in him may not perish but may have eternal life."[5] This is an oft-quoted verse but perhaps it means that Jesus offers a special relationship with God for those who wish to embrace that relationship. As I understand this statement, it definitely does not mean that God condemns the part of the "world" that does not proclaim Jesus as Logos or Son.

God wants to save the world, not condemn the world. When Jesus says, "I am the way," does he mean that he is the destination or that he is the *way*? I know people who do not profess Jesus as Savior, or Son, or Logos of God, who walk the way of Jesus better than some who profess the name of Jesus and who do not walk in the way of Jesus.

The Logos of God that was in Jesus of Nazareth is still very much alive and is a working force in the world, a world that God still loves and wants to save. Those Christians who are always talking about who will be "left behind" when an unbiblical rapture happens forget this important point. God still wants to save the world, not destroy it.

Perhaps the most pervasive kind of biblical malpractice comes from the supposed biblical underpinning in the *Left Behind* series of novels. These fictional stories are based on the misunderstandings of the "end times" that were propagated in the work of James Darby who came up with something called "dispensationalism."[6]

In order for this so-called rapture to take place, one has to believe that God is watching some timetable with certain trigger points that will set off a doomsday clock. The world will be in tribulation, and eventually the "bad" people will be destroyed. The "good" people will be "raptured," or lifted up, out of the path of this destruction. It matters not that there is no mention of such a rapture in the Bible, and that in any case, we are all a mixture of good and bad.

---

5. John 3:16.

6. To read more about this topic, see James M. Efird's book, *Left Behind? What the Bible Really Says About the End Times.*

Passages that are used to support the idea of rapture are metaphorical and are not meant to be taken literally. In First Thessalonians 4:17, for example, Paul tells us that those who are alive at the end will be "caught up in the clouds to meet the Lord in the air." Scholar and pastor James Efird points out that these words are pointing to a symbolic unity with God, and that this unity is described in spatial terms according to the understanding of that time.[7] "In case of Rapture, this car will be driverless" may make for a good bumper sticker, but it is not biblical.

I believe that the God of the Bible still wants the world to be saved. I also believe that the Spirit of Jesus is working within the Christian faith, in spite of certain forms of the Christian faith that diminish that Spirit. That same Spirit also works outside the Christian faith. God wants everyone home. God wants healing for the world. God wants the world to be saved, not destroyed. The Christ that I have encountered in my journey of faith is not one who would say "My way or the highway." The true Spirit of the Logos-made-flesh is a saving spirit not a destroying spirit.

The way of Christ is a wonderful way, but it is a difficult and challenging way of sacrificial love. As G. K. Chesterton once wrote in his book *What's Wrong with the World*, "The Christian ideal has not been tried and found wanting; it has been found difficult and left untried."[8] Jesus comes to offer the way, the truth, and the life. It is this way that can still lead to wholeness and healing, if tried. Some walk this way without using the name of Jesus. Others use the name of Jesus and come nowhere near walking his way. Which of these do you think God cares for more?

Remember that this book is written for the person who is not saying "no" to Jesus but who may be saying "no" to some of the beliefs about Jesus. It seems to me that if one studies the history of the Christian movement, what becomes apparent is that a few verses of Scripture have become the prism through which the whole faith is viewed.

7. Efird, *Left Behind*, 41.
8. Chesterton, *What's Wrong with the World*, 48.

The "only way" view has Jesus drawing a line in the sand and declaring that if a person does not believe that he is the only choice on the menu then sorry, but there is nothing else to eat, and the result is a slow starvation. What does this say about Jesus, and what kind of God would this be whom Jesus so intimately calls "Abba"?

This God would be a God who sent a child into the world to start nothing more than a club. The initiation rites for the club are a set of guidelines that center on ultimate allegiance to the originator of the club. This is not the picture of Jesus and his ministry that we see when we look at Scripture. Jesus was interested in tearing down walls, not building clubhouses. He spent most of his time with those who were excluded from the religious club of the day.

Right from the beginning of his ministry, Jesus was interested in opening up the club to new members, but the members would not have it. He selected as the board of directors for his new "organization" a group of people who did not measure up to the membership requirements for the existing club of the day. The club leaders accused Jesus of hanging out with those whom they termed "sinners," who are outsiders.

When Jesus made statements about being the "only way," he was contrasting his way with the way not only of a world that seemed lost, but a club that had become exclusive. Jesus said that the way to destruction is broad like a highway, but the way that leads to life is narrow like a path because it is not an easy place to walk, and it is off the beaten track of the world.

Examination of his path shows that it is a path of paying attention to the truly spiritual matters that affect temporal things, like who is hungry and who is outcast, and doing something about it. The broad highway is for people who want to build bigger barns to store their possessions and bigger clubhouses with higher walls and more stringent entrance requirements.

Jesus' way, once walked upon, leads around a corner where the path becomes more diverse because so many different kinds of people step upon it. He welcomed the people who were getting run over by the fast-paced people on the highway. Those were the hurried religious people who treated the very people Jesus welcomed as hitchhikers who did not deserve a ride.

Jesus got in trouble with those who at first thought he just might be the long-awaited new leader of the club who would bring the 2.0 version of new rules. Jesus did not bring a new set of rules and made a habit of picking up most every hitchhiker he passed. The closest he got to new rules had to do with blessing the poor, the rejected, the peacemakers, and those who were hurting.

His "only way" to the Father was more about announcing a new understanding of God that blew the minds of the very club that thought it had the copyright to market God. When the club discovered that Jesus was setting up roadside markets and almost giving away the products that bore God's name, they accused him of copyright violations. They also let him know in no uncertain terms that he was watering down the brand and lowering the quality of what it meant to be a club member.

The club started threatening him with all sorts of retaliation, and Jesus told them that they were acting like children who would not dance to the tune that was playing. Jesus would not dance to the religious music that the club was presenting as the only music to dance to. He said— and this really got him in trouble with the home office—that he was the Lord of the Dance and he wanted to offer music that the whole world could dance to.

The picture I am painting is of a Jesus who came for everybody, even those who do not dance to the particular religious music that is playing. He was about offering a way of life that leads to listening to people, listening to the birds of the air, considering the lilies of the field, and breaking down walls that separate people. Jesus came to offer a radical way of loving that involves risk. He did not offer a how-to-stay-safe manual for club members.

Personally I believe with all my heart that Jesus was the long-awaited Jewish Messiah. The Greek word for Messiah is Christ. It was not his last name. He came to offer a new way to the Hebrew people, but he discovered that the way of God had become a religious club. He turned over the tables at the club house, and the members quickly organized a committee to get rid of him. The committee succeeded, but the way of Jesus somehow could not be contained in the box in which they buried him.

All the titles used to describe Jesus may or may not be helpful if one decides to follow his radical way. They can sound like club officer titles if one stands outside his way and looks in. The titles can become simply labels for describing who is in and who is out. I do not believe that is what Jesus intends.

Yes, he is the Son of the living God in that he claims a special relationship to the "Father." At that time, "Son of God" was not a unique title. Caesar Augustus was also called the Son of God and Savior of the world.[9] Herod claimed to be the only King of the Jews that mattered. In the Jesus story, both of these powers tried to make sure that Jesus knew who was boss. They seemed to win and Jesus got crucified.

But hey, I am writing this, am I not? Caesar and Herod are ancient history while I profess and confess to you that to me, Jesus is Lord, King, Savior, and Son of God. What those titles mean to me cannot be contained in the index of a club membership manual. Jesus is Lord to me if I let him be. I try to rule over my own life often and want no one lording over me, but I get lost that way without something bigger guiding my path.

Jesus is King for me in that I need a ruler who cherishes my individuality while knowing that I need a kingdom to give myself to. Jesus is Savior to me because, quite frankly, I easily get lost in the jungle of self-preservation and need someone to remind me that it is not all about me. Jesus is Son of God but he is the son who felt lost and alone that night in the garden with all of his friends asleep when they were supposed to be looking out for the bad guys. Jesus knelt down and looked up and said something like, "Daddy, how about some help?"[10] Jesus brought us to us an understanding of a God who longs for a relationship with all God's children.

For you the reader, these titles will mean little if looked at as club titles. They are meant to be personal. The God of Jesus still cares about the salvation of the whole world, not just the club.

9. Erre, *The Jesus of Suburbia*, 7.
10. Matthew 26:39–42.

When the club spends its time studying copyright policy, the true mission of Jesus gets lost in the work of club meetings.

If I am wrong about this, and I could be, then I am in deep trouble according to those who believe that Jesus is the only way to salvation and all others are lost. In their eyes I am one of the lost. In that case, I will take my place with those who will be "left behind." I think you might just find Jesus at the end of the left-behind line. He was and is always looking for the lost.

12

Prayer

Is Prayer Really Talking to Yourself or to God? The Answer Is Yes

ANNE LAMOTT WRITES THAT there are basically three essential prayers: Help, Thanks, and Wow.[1] I suppose two of the three have to be directed to someone else. The "wow" can be done alone by simply pondering the wonder of life.

One of the problems with prayer is that it isn't what some people think it is. Prayer is not trying to convince a cosmic judge to offer a certain verdict. Prayer is not like an applause machine where, if enough people clap long and loud enough, the meter will suddenly read, "Okay already, you get what you want."

What kind of God would do something only if enough people prayed loud and long enough? And yet we seem to be a people who desire to have as many people joining us in a cause that we think is just. In our helplessness and our need to gain control when we do not have control, we gather people into our emotional auditorium and ask that people pray for the child who is struggling with cancer. We imply that if we get enough people signed up, our chances of winning the lottery go up. Is prayer for others like buying a lot of lottery tickets?

No wonder some people choose not to participate in religion. They would rather spend their money on a sure thing than the

1. Lamott, *Help, Thanks, Wow.*

chance option at the local church or the Seven Eleven store. They see the two institutions as places that offer the same thing.

Here is what Weatherhead writes:

> To pray for another is to expose both oneself and him to the common ground of our being: it is to see one's concern for him in terms of *ultimate* concern, to let *God* into the relationship. Intercession is to *be with* another at that depth, whether in silence or compassion or action. It may consist simply in listening, when we take the otherness of the other person most seriously. It may not be talking *to* God, as though to a third person, about him at all. The *Thou* addressed may be his own *Thou*, but it may be addressed and responded to at such a level that we can only speak of knowing him in God and God in him."[2]

So the title of this chapter is a question that leads to a paradox that is a both/and rather than an either/or. When we pray, we are with ourselves, and if God is not just a third party up there in the sky somewhere but an all-encompassing presence that is both within us and beyond us, then we are also with God.

For me prayer is a state of mind. When we attune our mind to something beyond the constant busyness that usually preoccupies our monkey mind, we make contact with something that is always there but not noticed. In his book *The Pleasure Prescription*, Paul Pearsall draws a distinction between the brain and the mind. He claims that our brain is the processing part of us but that our mind is the part of us that can stop and ponder the process. He goes on to say that one of the problems we face is that "our brain has lost its mind."[3]

Prayer at its core is first mindfulness before it is petition. In prayer we make contact with the ultimate being within us that comes from the ultimate being outside of us. Prayer puts us in contact with the beneath and the beyond.

At the core of reality is the mystery of being that is spirit. When we pray, we participate in the mystery. It is as if we take off

2. Weatherhead, *The Christian Agnostic*, 223.

3. Pearsall, *The Pleasure Prescription*, 28.

our shoes and stand barefoot in a flowing stream. As we do so we not only feel the water running over our feet but we also stand in the same water that is flowing over everyone's feet. We no longer are looking at others from the bank of the stream. We are *with* them and they are with us. Who knows what the touch, flow, and power of the water will do. But something happens that will not happen if we simply stand on the bank of the stream and observe or not observe.

I have prayed for many people in hospitals or Hospice houses. I have prayed in the home of a wife who just heard that her husband, the father of their two daughters, had been killed in an automobile accident. I have held onto two shocked and grieving parents as they faced the unexpected death of their beautiful teen-aged son. The list goes on.

So what am I doing when I pray? I am doing what I think spiritual beings who constantly face their limitations have to do. I am leaning into the mystery with the faith that someone more ultimate than I am is not only listening, but is with me, is with us. I am acknowledging that the presence that is always there is needed more than ever. I am affirming that the unseen—who is deeper and more real than the seen—needs to be experienced.

Even though I am a skeptic, I have learned that prayer changes me. Prayer does something to the pray-er. It makes sense that if we are spiritual beings then participating in a spiritual practice will affect us just as a physical exercise will affect our physical bodies.

To pray is to connect to that which breathes life into us. Paying attention to our breath is a basic form of prayer. To take that breath and form words is to take the next step. Those words can be in the form of blessing people or asking something for them. Somehow the universe is altered when we care enough to pray.

When something on the outside is altered when we pray, or because we pray, it is not because the needle on the applause meter is moved. When we pray, we step into a source of power that is within the universe. Some of that power is within us. To pray is to align our power with *the* power. It is not a one-to-one relationship.

To pray is not to do some cosmic math equation. To pray is to step into the mystery not knowing how the end will add up.

But I believe something does happen when we pray. Whatever it is cannot be packaged, as some religion claims it to be. Such packaging leads to those crass understandings of prayer that lead many people to believe that prayer is nothing more than self-talk that is obviously not overheard by the "man upstairs" because most of the time the pray-er does not get the desired result.

As one irate wife shouted at me when her husband left her without a word, "Don't you give me that crap about prayer. I've already tried it and no one was at home when I knocked." Jesus tells stories that portray the reality that someone is always home but that you still may not get what you want. Prayer is not a knock knock joke.

God is always there, but God is not Santa Claus behind the door. God is the mysterious stream we step into. Prayer simply must be done, not just thought about. The stream I keep mentioning runs throughout the universe.

The universe is more of a loving idea than it is a machine. In his book *God According to God*, Gerald Schroeder, a physicist, puts forward the idea, voiced also by other eminent physicists, that there is a reality even deeper than the fields and forces of the subatomic world. He speculates that mind is the source of matter. He writes, "Suddenly the old conundrum of how the physical brain gives rise to the ethereal mind and experienced sentience evaporates. It is not a question of consciousness arising from matter. It is rather the opposite, of matter arising from consciousness."[4]

Schroeder further comments that:

> The diversity of the cosmos, built of time and space and matter, has arisen from a singularity, not of the physical type couched within a black hole, but of a unity brought into being as mind, the first act of the creation. And the wisdom of our minds, if used properly, can close the loop, linking with this underlying mind of creation.[5]

4. Schroeder, *God According to God*, 226.
5. Ibid., 227.

Schroeder closes his book by quoting the words of John Archibald Wheeler, the former President of the American Physical Society, who participated in a BBC special entitled *The Creation of the Universe:*

> To my mind, there must be at the bottom of it all, not an utterly simple equation, but an utterly simple IDEA. And to me that idea, when we finally discover it, will be so compelling, and so inevitable, so beautiful, we will say to each other, "How could it have ever been otherwise?"[6]

To pray is to participate in the holy idea that is the mind of the universe. We are not standing before a cosmic applause meter nor are we peering into a vacant and mechanistic abyss. We are standing in the flowing stream of spirit. As we stand with our shoes off in the stream, the flow of the water is altered and we are touched by the constant motion of life.

Our minds connect to an ultimate mind whose idea it was to create life. We are in that moment with ourselves and with the idea that created us and everything else. And yes, in that moment of standing within the ultimate we too can whisper, "What a wonderful idea . . . thanks . . . wow . . . and help."

6. Ibid.

A Sort of Creed for
a Christian Skeptic

SINCE THIS BOOK WAS inspired by Leslie Weatherhead's book *The Christian Agnostic*, and my title contains within it the struggle to believe, I offer now a kind of affirmation of faith for the person who says, "I believe; help my unbelief!"

I BELIEVE; HELP MY UNBELIEF!

I believe in God,
or, at least, I want to believe.
I believe that God is bigger than my feelings about God;
there are times I do not feel God's presence,
yet I believe God is still there.
I believe that God is mostly made up of mystery
and that I can only know a portion of what God is,
but that is enough.
I believe that God must want us to know as much as we can about
God,
about the created order,
and about ourselves.
I believe that God holds both life and death
and that some things I will only understand
on the other side of life.

I believe in Jesus,
but not the one on bumper stickers.

I believe that Jesus was divine
because he was fully human.
I believe that Jesus invites me to be fully human
by inviting me to be more like him.
I believe that being like him requires
a new way of life that involves radical loving.
I believe that Jesus offered his life
so that all of life could be different,
but it will not be different
unless I follow in his ways,
rather than just use his name.
I believe that Jesus somehow overcame death,
but I am not sure how.
Therefore I believe that resurrection
is a mystery to be embraced,
rather than a doctrine to be understood.

I believe in a power called the Holy Spirit
that is as close as my next breath
because it is the breath of life.
I believe that whatever the Holy Spirit is,
it fills all of life and creates something
we call beauty.
I believe that the Holy Spirit is working
to heal a world that is broken
and that, if I will cooperate with this Spirit,
healing can happen
in my life and in the world.
I believe that, because the Holy Spirit is in everyone,
everyone is a child of God
and should be treated that way.

I believe that the church is not a building,
but a community
of those who attempt to follow in the way of Jesus.
I believe that the church often fails to follow Jesus

but that Jesus will not give up on the church
or give up on the world that the church is called to transform.
I believe that the church is one place
that the story of Jesus
is not just to be told,
but to be lived, and that happens
when the story is proclaimed and enacted
through word and ritual.

I believe; help my unbelief!
for I believe that God is more interested in my journey
than in my destination.
But I also believe that my journey began with God
and that my ultimate destination will again
be with God.

Bibliography

Amichai, Yehuda. *The Selected Poetry of Yehuda Amichai*, translated by Chana Bloch and Stephen Mitchell. Berkley and Los Angeles, CA: University of California Press, 1986.

Armstrong, Karen. *The Bible: A Biography.* New York, NY: Atlantic Monthly, 2007.

Bell, Martin. *The Way of the Wolf: The Gospel in New Images.* New York, NY: Ballantine Books, 1970.

Bell, Rob. *Love Wins: A Book about Heaven, Hell, and the Fate of Every Person Who Lived.* New York, NY: HarperOne, 2005.

Berger, Peter L. *A Rumour of Angels: Modern Society and the Rediscovery of the Supernatural.* Garden City, NY: Anchor, 1970.

Borg, Marcus. *The Heart of Christianity: Rediscovering a Life of Faith.* New York, NY: HarperCollins, 2003.

Buechner, Frederick. *The Hungering Dark.* New York, NY: HarperCollins, 1969.

Burke, Spencer. *A Heretic's Guide to Eternity,* by Spencer Burke and Barry Taylor. San Francisco, CA: Jossey-Bass, 2006.

Cannon, Mae Elise. *Social Justice Handbook: Small Steps for a Better World.* Foreword by John Perkins. Downers Grove, IL: InterVarsity, 2009.

Caroll, Sean. *The Particle at the End of the Universe: How the Hunt for the Higgs Bosun Leads Us to the Edge of a New World.* New York, NY: Penguin, 2012.

Chesterton, G.K. *What's Wrong with the World.* Fort Collins, CO: Ignatius Press, 1994.

Cobb, John B. *The Process Perspective: Frequently Asked Questions about Process Theology.* St. Louis, MO: Chalice Press, 2003.

Collins, Francis S. *The Language of God: A Scientist Presents Evidence for the Bible.* New York, NY: Free Press, 2006.

Efird, James M. *Left Behind? What the Bible Really Says about the End Times.* Macon, GA: Smyth & Helwys, 2006.

Eliot, T.S. "Little Gidding," in *The Norton Anthology of Modern Poetry,* edited by Richard Ellman and Robert O'Clair. New York, NY: Norton, 1973.

Erre, Mike. *The Jesus of Suburbia: Have we tamed the Son of God to Fit our Lifestyle?* Nashville, TN: Thomas Nelson, 2006.

Fox, Matthew. *The Coming of the Cosmic Christ: The Healing of Mother Earth and the Birth of a Global Renaissance.* New York, NY: HarperCollins, 1988.

Hankey, Katherine. "I love to tell the story," in *The United Methodist Hymnal: Book of United Methodist Worship*. Nashville, TN: The United Methodist Publishing House, 1989.

Heim, Mark. *Saved from Sacrifice: A Theology of the Cross*. Grand Rapids, MI: Wm B. Eerdmans, 2006.

Hollis, James. *Tracking the Gods: The Place of Myth in Modern Life*, Toronto: Inner City Books, 1995.

Homer. *The Odyssey*, translated by Robert Fagles, introduction and notes by Bernard Knox. New York, NY: Penguin, 1996.

Huxley, T.H. *T.H. Huxley on Education: A Selection from his Writings*, introduction by Cyril Bibby. Cambridge, UK: Cambridge University Press, 1971.

Jacobs, Anton K. *Religion and the Critical Mind: A Journey for Seekers, Doubters, and the Curious*. Lanham, MD: Lexington Books, 2010.

Jones, Tony. *The New Christians: Dispatches from the Emergent Frontier*. San Francisco, CA: Jossey-Bass, 2008.

Kierkegaard Søren. *The Essential Kierkegaard*, Princeton, NJ: Princeton University Press, 2000.

———. *Fear and Trembling*, edited by C. Stephen Evans and Sylvia Walsh. Cambridge, UK: Cambridge University Press, 2006.

———. *Philosophical Fragments*. Princeton, NJ: Princeton University Press, 1962.

———. *The Last Years: The Kierkegaard Journals, 1853–1855*. Collins/Fontana, 1968.

———. *The Soul of Kierkegaard: Selections from his Journal*, edited and with an introduction by Alexander Dru. Mineola, NY: Dover, 2003.

Kilbourne, Ed. *The Best of Ed Kilbourne*. Rock Hill, SC: Fly-By-Night Records, 1998.

Kushner, Harold S. *When Bad Things Happen to Good People*. New York, NY: Random House, 1981.

Lamott, Anne. *Help, Thanks, Wow: The Three Essential Prayers*. New York, NY: Penguin, 2012.

———. *Plan B: Further Thoughts on Faith*. New York, NY: Berkley Publishing Group, 2005.

Linafelt, Tod. *Shadow of Glory: Reading the New Testament after the Holocaust*. New York, NY: Routledge, 2002.

Luther, Martin. *The Prefaces to the Early Editions of Martin Luther's Bible*, edited by T.A. Redwin. London: Hatchard and Co., 1863.

Markham, Edwin. *New Poems: Eighty Songs at Eighty. The Fifth Book of Verse*. Garden City, NY: Doubleday, Doran & Company, 1932.

McLaren, Brian D. *A Generous Orthodoxy*. Grand Rapids, MI: Zondervan, 2004.

———. *A New Kind of Christianity: Ten Questions that Are Transforming the Faith*. New York, NY: HarperOne, 2010.

Marsh, Donald Stuart, and Avery, Richard Kinsey. "The Holy Spirit and Elmer's Glue." Hope Publishing Company, 1973.

Mesle, C. Robert. *Process Theology: A Basic Introduction*. Danvers, MA: Chalice Press, 1993.

Meyers, Robin R. *Saving Jesus from the Church: How to Stop Worshiping Christ and Start Following Jesus*. New York, NY: HarperCollins, 2009.

Otto, Rudolph. *The Idea of the Holy*. Oxford, UK: Oxford University Press, 1958.

Pearsall, Paul. *The Pleasure Prescription: To Love, to Work, to Play – Life in the Balance*. Salt Lake City, UT: Publishers Press, 1996.

Pelikan, Jaroslav. *The Illustrated Jesus through the Centuries*. New Haven: Yale University Press, 1997.

Phillips, J.B. *Your God Is Too Small*. New York, NY: Macmillan, 1952.

Prothero, Stephen. *American Jesus: How the Son of God Became a National Icon*, New York, NY: Farrar, Straus and Giroux, 2003.

Rees, Frank D. *Wrestling with Doubt*. Collegeville, MN: The Order of St. Benedict, 2001.

Rilke, Rainer Maria. *Letters to a Young Poet*, translated, edited and with notes and an afterward by Charlie Louth, introduction by Lewis Hyde. New York, NY: Penguin, 2013.

Rohr, Richard. *Falling Upward: A Spirituality for the Two Halves of Life*. San Francisco, CA: Jossey-Bass, 2011.

―――. *Immortal Diamond: The Search for our True Self*. San Francisco, CA: Jossey-Bass, 2013.

Schroeder, Gerald. *God According to God: A Physicist Proves We've Been Wrong about God All Along*. New York, NY: HarperCollins, 2009.

―――. *The Science of God: The Convergence of Scientific and Biblical Wisdom*. New York, NY: Bantam Doubleday Dell, 1997.

Schweitzer, Albert. *The Quest of the Historical Jesus*, translated W. Montgomery. New York, NY: MacMillan, 1968.

Tillich, Paul. *Paul Tillich: Theologian of the Boundaries*, edited by Mark Kline Taylor. Minneapolis, MN: Augsburg Fortress, 1991.

Turner, Alice K. *The History of Hell*. Orlando, FL: Harcourt, Brace & Company, 1993.

The United Methodist Church. *The Book of Discipline of the United Methodist Church 2012*. Nashville, TN: The United Methodist Publishing House, 2012.

Wald, George, "Life and Mind in the Universe," from *The International Journal of Quantum Chemistry: Quantum Biology*, symposium 11 (1984).

Weatherhead, Leslie D. *The Christian Agnostic*. New York, NY: Abingdon, 1965.

―――. *The Will of God*. Nashville, TN: Abingdon, 1944.

Whitehead, Alfred North. *Religion in the Making: Lowell Lectures, 1926*. New York, NY: Fordham University Press, 1996.

Young, William P. *The Shack*. Newbury Park, CA: Windblown Media, 2007.

Lightning Source UK Ltd.
Milton Keynes UK
UKOW05f0654260117
292853UK00001B/152/P